Divorce Happens:
Bounce Back!

Tasfil Publishing, LLC

New Jersey, USA
www.tasfil.com

The author of this book does not dispense medical advice or prescribe the use of any technique as a form of treatment for physical, emotional, or medical problems without the advice of a physician, either directly or indirectly. The intent of the author is only to offer information of a general nature to help you in your quest for emotional or spiritual well-being. In the event you use any of the information in this book for yourself, which is your constitutional right, the author and publisher assume no responsibility for your actions.

Editor's Note: In order to avoid awkward "he/she," "him/her" references, the plural "they" or "their" has often been used to refer to singular antecedents such as "person" or "partner" even though this construction doesn't adhere to strict grammatical rules.

Cover Design: Laura Jacoby

Cover Photography: Dana Romano Photography

ISBN: 09862580-2-2
ISBN-13 978-0986258022

Other books by this author:

Life Happens: Bounce Back!

Dedication

This book is dedicated to my sons, Jacob and Ari.

You are my heart, light, and the greatest gift I have ever received.

It's an honor and a privilege to be your mom.

I hope as you go through life, you will always bounce back
with laughter and love.

This book recounts incidents, people and places in my life according to my recollection of the events. I have related them to the best of my knowledge. I have also changed the identities of the people involved or created composites of them to protect their right to privacy.

Why I wrote this book!

Sometimes we forget why we decided to do things. This book, for example. I decided years ago, after my second marriage ended, that someone needed to write a book to help people put their life back together after a divorce, a short book that hits on the main things that matter the most. By the time I realized I was going to do it myself, I had healed enough that I'd forgotten why I had made the decision as I focused on following through on it. But today, January 12, 2015, I was given a stark reminder.

I took part in a round-table discussion to help women face their fear of divorce. As we spoke about the general to-do list of divorce—finding the right attorney, choosing between renting or buying a new home, etc.—the pain and gut-wrenching reality of the situation shook my body, as if I were experiencing the dissolution of a marriage all over again. Everything felt so very scary and overwhelming. "Divorce can rock your world," as one of my friends said it best. It's change and fear all wrapped into one big ball in the pit of your stomach.

Leaving the event, on this dreary day, I thought to myself, *Oh my God! I cannot believe I lived through so much pain and unhappiness.* And, to be perfectly honest, lots of ugliness, too. I came home intent on doing some self-care for me. I lit a few candles and made myself a nice cup of hot chocolate, topped off with tiny marshmallows. Then I sat quietly to reflect on my morning.

I realized that today, almost sixteen years after my first divorce, and six years after my second, I was more convinced than ever that *everyone* needs to be reminded about the light at the end of the tunnel. Not only needed to be reminded, but given a little help along the path.

So that's one reason why I wrote this book.

The other is to remind you that you do not have to go through this devastating time alone.

When I divorced, both times I was blessed with the most amazing support system; my parents, my family and friends never stopped supporting me. My friend Vicky was there 24/7 after my first divorce. I remember sleeping on her couch when my son was at his dad's because I just could not deal with the pain, the empty feeling of facing the fear and being alone.

My second divorce also included filing for personal bankruptcy, losing my job and starting my own business. Talk about fear on overdrive.

In other words, I know what you're going through.

After I made it through, I made a promise that anyone in need of extra love, time or attention while going through a divorce would get it from me. Anytime I hear someone is thinking about getting a divorce, or going through it, I am the first one to offer my ear. It's my way of paying it forward for all the love and support I received so unconditionally from my family and friends.

I promise you, there is a light. So try every day to lift your head and hold it high. Remember, in the end, you *will* be better because of this divorce. I promise you, this is part of your life's journey. You will learn and grow in ways you never imagined you could.

It's not an easy road. It will be longer for some of you than for others. But, if you educate yourself and surround yourself with a team of people who support you, you will be okay. I realize that some of you may feel as if you are alone and you may be wondering if you can make it without a team. If that is the case, please believe me: you are never truly alone. There are support groups and organizations out there that can help you. Do an internet search, ask your physician, check out community centers. If you force yourself to reach out, you may just be pleasantly surprised by what you will find.

Life happens, and we can all bounce back.

Divorce happens, too. And you can bounce back from it!

Table of Contents

Divorce Happens:

Bounce Back!

Believe in yourself
and the rest
of your life
will fall into place.

Introduction

Oh my God! Really? You're getting a divorce? Why? What happened?

That is pretty much the initial reaction you get when you tell someone you are getting divorced. Everyone is so curious about the *why*?

Sometimes I think people want to know *why* so that maybe they can prevent it from happening to them. As if divorce was a disease. Of course if it were, things would be so much simpler. Wouldn't it be great if there was a prescription you could take to fix an unhappy marriage? *Here: take this tablet once a day and you will be relieved of all your frustration and unhappiness.* There would be a market for that pill, I'm sure.

At other times, though, I feel like screaming: "Who cares why? *Why* doesn't matter!" In my opinion, when two people decide to get a divorce and they tell their family and friends, it is not time for: *Why?* It is time for: *It will be okay. We love you and we are here for you.* Hopefully, if you're not getting the right support from the people around you, you will get it from me in this book.

Even though everyone handles it differently and is impacted by it differently, divorce is an incredibly overwhelming and scary time for everyone. So, if you are considering a divorce, going through one, or are divorced and just need some reassurance about how good life can be, this book is for you. And my first advice to you now is to breathe, smile, and trust me when I say: things can be great again. They really can.

Divorce is an end and a beginning–an end to a relationship and a beginning to a beautiful new life. One that *you* get to design! If you take the time to learn from the pain and dig deep into the reasons your marriage really ended, I promise you, you will find a happier ever after; it will be with *yourself*. You can have the greatest love affair of all time with yourself. I know it's possible because that's exactly what I've done.

Life is not always easy. But as life happens, we can always bounce back. We all go through tough times and divorce, with -or without children, is just that: a tough time. A really tough time. Divorce is like a death. It can leave us with an empty feeling that can linger for a very long time.

Please keep this in mind: how long the sadness and negative emotions linger, is really up to you. It is up to you how long you stay connected to the hurt and the pain. Likewise, it is up to you to decide when it is time to cut the cord connecting you to the bad stuff.

It makes me sad when I hear people talking about their ex- in a negative way. In turn it makes me sadder when I see people cannot move on because they continue to hold on to the pain and the feelings of loss. It's just not necessary. You can find happiness again.

This book explains how I managed to go from believing I was an absolute failure to being at peace with my divorces. I explain how I've learned to view marriage and divorce, and I share with you the perspective I've gained from my experiences with the hope that you can learn from my example. I also go into a frank and open discussion about the initial shock and trauma many of us go through with our divorces and provide a little insight to help you learn to better deal with the emotional ups and downs.

I talk about what I consider to be key elements for living your post-divorce life in as emotionally and mentally healthy manner possible for you, your children and even for your ex-spouse. We all thought marriage would take us down the yellow brick road and we would find our pot of gold with our spouse, new home, two kids, a mini-van but...WAIT! Your life didn't work out that way. So, if marriage is not the end-all and be-all, I guess divorce is not the doom-and-gloom picture so many see it as. I explain my four-step bounce-back plan that, when you're ready, will help you bounce back from your divorce and start actively living your life with joy and passion again.

Finally, in the last chapters I've asked a couple of experts to offer their wisdom. You'll get sound advice from an attorney and an accountant and you'll be inspired by some personal tales from women who discovered true joy and happiness after their divorces.

But, before we get into the nitty-gritty of how to heal and move on to a better life after your divorce, let's clarify what I mean when I talk about love and marriage. Many people *think* they know what it means to be married or what it means to be divorced, but seldom do they ever really get to the bottom of what either means to them personally, because they're too caught up in emotions or believing in ideals.

However, you can't really heal and move on until you realize exactly what it is you're in need of healing from. Frankly, I didn't even think about what it meant to be married, nor what it meant to be divorced, until *after* my second marriage ended. And it was only when I stopped to think about it all that I understood the whole truth behind why my marriages ended. Not only that, but that's when I discovered how to bounce back from my divorces and start living an authentically happy life.

So, let's start at the beginning and ask: *what does it really mean to be married?*

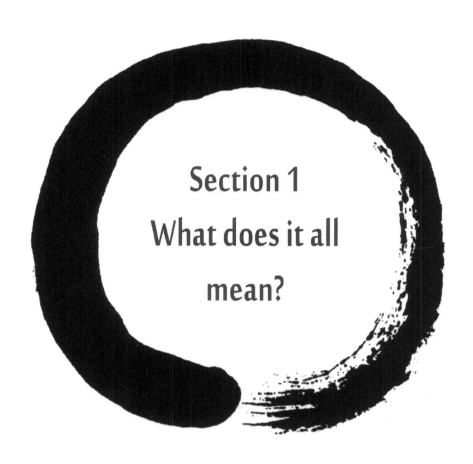

Section 1
What does it all
mean?

Chapter 1:
What Marriage Means to Me

Love and Marriage

I love the idea of marriage. But, like I said, I never stopped to think about what it really meant to be married. Ask yourself now: *really, what is marriage?*

Is marriage a commitment? A friendship of two people who will work hard to make their commitment to each other last a lifetime no matter what?

Here is my definition of marriage: It's a partnership. It's teamwork. It's two people making each other better through their mutual love and respect for each other. I feel there must be respect for each other because when the lust goes away, or should the physical attraction fade, there needs to be something else there to keep the people together. In a healthy marriage, when you are together, you are the best version of you, and when separate, you are still you and just knowing you have the love of your partner makes you want to be even better.

To me, you should always strive to be the best version of you–marriage should enhance that spirit with a feeling of oneness.

Why Do People Get Married

So why do people get married? Is it because they love each other? Is love really enough? What if there are fundamental differences between them? Can love truly conquer all? I don't think that last one can be answered with *yes*. In fact, I think maybe we should be asking: why are there so many divorces? Why do we all know people who have been through them?

Couples walk down the aisle starry eyed, optimistic that their marriage will last forever, and then years later *boom*! What causes the boom? Is it really: *he did this,* or *she did that* and it's off to the lawyer we go? No. It's just not that simple, I know.

After my first divorce, my aunt said, "I knew it was not going to last." At first I asked her how she knew, but then I was more interested in knowing why she never said anything to me.

Actually, the truth of the matter is that many people did say something about my pending first marriage. In fact, my mom and dad sat me down, questioned me, and asked me to rethink my decision. My family knew there were too many differences between my fiancé and me. I don't now, and will never, regret my marriages to either of my ex-husbands because I have my two wonderful boys. But, whenever asked, my advice to people who are thinking about getting married is always: notice the differences you may have with your fiancé. Make sure they don't have potential to eventually be deal- breakers. Pay attention to the red flags–they're not part of a parade, they are warning signs.

What's Love Got to Do with It?

I remember asking my aunt why her marriage to my uncle Ted lasted 55 years and was still going strong. I wanted the "recipe" or the "secret" to being happily married. She said love had nothing to do with it.

Sure, she loved him, but the real reason their marriage was so successful, my aunt explained, is that their lifestyles matched. She was able to embrace his success and the work schedule that required him to travel a great deal. Wow! I still remember hearing those words: *love had nothing to do with it*.

So there you have it: *love* is not the key ingredient to a long-lasting, healthy marriage.

I clearly did not know that going into either of my marriages. I knew I had issues or differences with both men, but I believed each time that we loved each other enough to work through them. I clearly remember me saying to a dear friend before my second marriage that I did not think you can have it all: "No man has everything you want, so you must compromise."

In hindsight, I think I misinterpreted "compromise" to mean "settle." Settling is seldom a good idea in a marriage. Settling can lead to disappointment, resentment, anger and a whole host of negative emotions that can damage or even destroy your marriage.

My first husband was not Jewish. I am. In the beginning, I didn't think our different faiths would be an issue. After all, there were probably thousands, if not millions, of interfaith couples in the world who were able to make it work. Why couldn't we? Well, the difference for us was too big. Or maybe it was just one of too many differences, I don't know. But the fact that I missed sharing the holidays with someone who embraced them as I did, was one of the first things to drive a wedge between my husband and me.

It was different with my second husband. We got along great all the time, like the good friends we continue to be. Unfortunately we had no chemistry. I figured the chemistry would eventually come. But it didn't.

"The Talk"

In a perfect world we would have all the answers before we needed them. There would always be someone to sit us down and give us a talk explaining what we needed to know for every situation ahead of time. But since the world's not perfect, it's up to each of us to try to make sure we don't walk in to any situation blindfolded. I guess we gotta give ourselves that talk as best as we can by taking clues from what has worked, and not, for ourselves in the past and even for others in similar circumstances.

When I was young girl, I truly believed you grew up, fell in love (though I had no clue what that meant), got married and stayed married 'til death do you part. That was how you lived happily ever after.

In fact, I remember one day in high school when my gym teacher and I were talking. He asked me what I wanted to do when I grew up. I said, "Get married and be a mom." "No, really," he said. "Besides that, what do you want to do?" I responded again: "Get married and be a mom."

I was raised to believe that if you get a good education, get your college degree, and get married, then you will live happily ever after. Even after my first marriage broke up, I still believed that's what you did. You just needed to find a spouse you could compromise with.

Looking back, I still believe you have to compromise a lot to be committed to the idea of being committed, but, and here is the big BUT: You must compromise, not settle. Before you get married, you must decide what is important to you and what are some of your *must haves* in a relationship, not just a marriage, and don't settle for anything less.

9

> I am now very clear on my must haves for my next boyfriend and one-day life partner. My next partner must be very curious about life, like I am. A sense of humor is key. A big heart and a passion for life are too; after all, how can I share my passion with someone who wants to sit on the couch and watch other people live? Recently I asked a man about attending an opera. I said, "Would you go?" He said, "I will try anything once. I am open to it!" Now, *that* is a good answer. Curiosity is important to me. I love life and want someone who is enthusiastic and willing to grow with me. And I want someone to stand next to me so we can support each other on a daily basis and be each other's cheerleaders.

Right now, if your divorce isn't final or if it's still too fresh, you might not be in the right place to figure out what kind of person your ideal partner would be. But it is the perfect time to figure out what marriage means to you for a couple reasons.

The first reason is so you can see exactly *which* of your differences played a part in your marriage breaking up. If you don't understand what is necessary in a good marriage for you, after your divorce, you may end up repeating the same mistakes with a new partner.

The second reason is that you can heal and recover from a broken marriage only if you completely understand why it fell apart. If you stay stuck in *he did this to us* or *it's all her fault,* you will never be able to bounce back.

My hope is that by sharing what I've learned from my experiences, I can help you bounce back and become happier than you ever have been. And the first thing I did was to figure out what marriage meant to me. The second thing I did was to figure out what it meant to be divorced.

Chapter 2:
What Divorce Means to Me

It's A Matter of Circumstance

I guess you could say that I had gotten married for the wrong reasons. I think that's something many people do. But you know what? Some people get married for all the right reasons, or so it appears, and their marriage does not work out either. It is a crap shoot in the end.

And perhaps that's the perfect metaphor for when it comes to picking a partner to stay with for the rest of your life. Choosing someone 'til death do you part is a gamble. No one truly knows if, in the end, it will work and last forever. Seriously, we are human beings and we change and evolve every day. How can someone possibly believe she will be married to one man for the rest of her life?

Do I sound cynical? Maybe I am a little cynical, but here is what I do believe: if you know who you are at the time you decide to get married, you make the best decision based on facts and not purely on emotion (or hot sex), you are willing to work hard to make it work, and you are committed to being committed, then you have a good shot of being in a marriage that lasts.

Unfortunately, most of us are too young, inexperienced, naïve, or _____ (fill in the blank) to have the setup be ideal. Instead, we think we have a perfect combination of character traits with our partner (there is no such thing) or that we'll discover the one secret to a lifetime of marriage bliss (ditto). We are human beings living wonderful human experiences. Sometimes that is hard enough to do by yourself so when you throw a partner into the mix, well, it can make things too complicated. Life is an ongoing work-in-progress. If we could all understand that we are continually evolving and that our relationships are designed to ebb and flow as we grow, we would all be able to deal with the ups and downs of relationships. We could all understand that relationships end due to circumstances, not to someone failing.

The Call from Your Attorney–The Sigh of Relief, or Not

I remember the night my attorney called to say my first ex-husband and I had reached an agreement. All we needed to do was wait for the court document to arrive. I was as good as done. WOW! What relief–like a big weight had been lifted off my back, one that had been there for years.

When the second one ended, though, it was another story. Before I even started the divorce proceedings, I was too embarrassed for a very long time to even admit that I was getting a divorce. That guilt weighed me down like a big brick attached to a neon sign hanging over my headed screaming: "LOSER!"

Yes, loser. I was so disappointed in myself. I had wanted the perfect family. Like I said earlier, when I got married the first time I truly believed 'til death do us part. I wanted nothing more than to live that dream of happily ever after. Of growing old with my husband. Of having a baby and raising our child in a secure world full of the love of his mom and dad, with everyone living under one roof. You know, my version (at the time) of what a "real" family should be like.

Unfortunately, I held on to that idea when I tried marriage the second time.

So getting divorce number two was like torture for me. At that time, both of my older brothers were happily married and I kept thinking, *Here I go again. The youngest equals the failure.*

I had myself so convinced that divorce would define me as a failure that I hid the truth for as long as I could. I pretended I was happily married for far too long. I couldn't understand how I could have screwed up so badly that I was getting a divorce, again. I didn't think to myself, *I bet you're not the only one going through this.* No. I could only think that I was a failure. Not only had I failed at marriage, but I had failed as a mom. I thought my sons deserved more and better than having their parents divorce. To me, they were being cheated out on a "real" family and it was *all my fault.* If I hadn't failed, they would have gotten what they deserved.

But today, I know the truth. My divorce is not a failure on anyone's part. It was just an end to a relationship that did not work out. Because that's what divorce simply is: an end to a relationship that did not work out.

Let me repeat that: divorce is simply an end to a relationship that did not work out.

There is no need to blame one person or the other–the truth of the matter is that sometimes relationships just don't work.

And now I also understand that the worry I had about cheating my sons out of a real family was completely unnecessary. They were never cheated out of anything. We created a family that involved extended family, a step-father, a younger brother and a lot of friends who constantly surround my sons with unconditional love and support.

Divorce Does Not Define You

Of course I didn't just wake up one day being at peace with my divorces. It took me awhile and it didn't begin until I realized my divorce didn't define me. I am always more than a situation. You, too, are always more than a situation.

It wasn't easy for me to believe that. I had to remind myself daily. *Divorce does not define who I am–it's an outcome from an experience that did not work* became my mantra.

In fact, divorce is just *one thing* that can happen after two people fall in love and decide to spend the rest of their lives together. We all know the ideal path: get married, buy a house and start a family. But like with most paths in life, there are many ways to branch off of it. Creating a nuclear family is just one path. Remaining childless in a lofted apartment in Manhattan is another. Staying single all your life is yet another. And so is getting a divorce. There are many different paths available to us. Not only that, but we have the freedom to change our minds as we go down them. We are not the paths. Our paths do not define us. Our paths are simply situations and circumstances we experience.

So while initially I felt like a failure because my marriages didn't work, eventually I realized the truth: both divorces were outcomes. They were outcomes of marriages where there was a *major disconnect*, where there were large *differences*, between the spouses. The divorces didn't say anything about me, personally. But they said quite a bit about the marriages.

Ex-husband number one

My first marriage was exciting. I married a rough, tough half-Italian and half-Irish man. I was always, and continue to be, a fan of Italian men. On top of that, he was a bit of a "bad" boy. And I had always been attracted to the "bad" boys.

No one wanted me to marry him. But what does a girl do when people say, "No! Don't marry him!"? She runs right into his arms.

I was young and immature and just wanted to be married. It's true–I admit it–I just wanted to be married so badly that I thought *why not?* He was cute, good in bed, fun and liked to party like me. Plus, I loved his family. Looking back now, I can see there were too many differences. We were not a good fit. Though I will never regret my marriage to him. Because of that union, our son Jacob was born. He is a light in my life.

Ex-husband number two

My second husband, Richard, was a sweet, wonderful man, and continues to be. He and I are great friends and the million dollar question of the day is always the same: *why are the two of you not together?* It's simple. He drives me crazy. I love him as a friend. We just never had any chemistry.

When we tried marriage counseling the counselor asked me: "When you first met was there chemistry?" I said, "No." She responded with: "What makes you think that now, six years later, you would have it?"

I couldn't answer her.

So in hindsight, I can see that no one failed in either of my marriages. The situations just contained too many large differences for us to be able to bridge. I will not go into all the particulars of my marriages, what purpose would that serve? The goal of the book is not to rehash my past relationships, but instead it is intended to remind everyone that what we believed something was, and what it actually was (or is), can be two very different things.

Both my marriages ended due to differences that we should have recognized from the beginning. It's true that some differences can be ignored. Sometimes they can even add spice to your married life. But when they are too great, or too many, the differences can take over and instead of enhancing the married life, they destroy it. And that's what divorce means to me: a marriage where the differences take over and the two people decide to go their own ways.

I am sure some of you are reading this and thinking there has to be more to it. I can hear you now: *My ex- cheated on me!* Or *He had a gambling problem that put us into foreclosure.* Or *She insisted on her mother moving in . . .*

I understand all those situations on the surface look like someone did something that ultimately caused the marriage to break apart. But I promise you, if you look a little deeper, you'll discover at the root of each one, there were differences between the spouses that grew over time to the point of being unbridgeable. Think about it: not every marriage that suffers similar problems comes to an end. Some couples are able to get to the root of their problems, fix them and have even better marriages afterward. That's another path.

> **This seems like a good time to share my views on extramarital indiscretions. When someone cheats on their spouse they are not cheating on you–they are cheating on themselves. Remember that, there are two types of cheating: emotional and physical. I am not sure which is worse; that is a personal decision. The act of sex is just that: sex. So, I think the emotional attachment is more painful and a greater cheat. For me, if someone cheats on me with an emotional relationship that is more painful than a physical relationship. But, here is my theory on this one, ready? They go hand in hand sometimes. We confuse sex with emotion and then the emotion causes us to have the sex and we think it's the best sex ever. You all know what I am talking about. We all say, *OMG that was the best sex ever* when we are totally 100% connected with our partner. The stronger the emotional attachment I have, the better the sex. Not a news flash I am sure to some, but it is true. And, it took me a long time to buy into it, but it's true.**

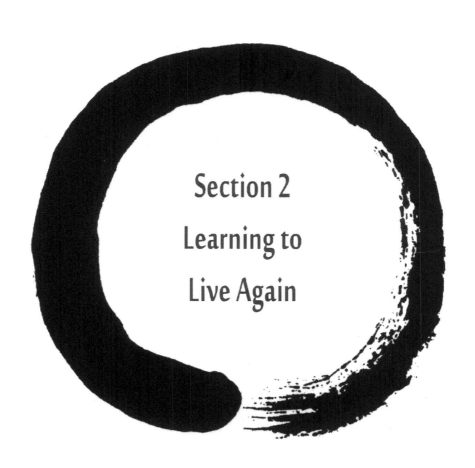

Section 2

Learning to

Live Again

Chapter 3:
Getting Over the Initial Shock

The Stigma Is Gone

The funny thing about divorce is that, although it's common to feel like a failure because you get one, no one else will bat an eye about it. The stigma is gone.

I love to discuss the topic of divorce and hear other people's opinions on it. Recently, I found myself laughing with someone as I explained I had been married and divorced twice. It's like it was no big deal–because it is no big deal!

Yes, there was once a stigma connected to being divorced. But now, not only has it become commonplace, it is almost a badge of honor: *Oh, so you are divorced?* It means you've been through a tough time and came out on the other side. It means you're strong. It means you know what you can handle; that you've figured out what's best for you.

My friends and I have even said that we would rather date someone who was married and divorced, versus someone who is over forty and never married.

So keep that in mind if you're having problems feeling like a failure or if you're worried about how other people will perceive you when you tell them that you're getting a divorce or that you are divorced. Few people will see it as negatively as you do.

Happiness After Divorce

Perhaps one of the reasons why divorce is seen in such a positive light by many people is because there are several living examples of how men and women are happier with their lives post divorce.

Recently, I was talking to a woman in her seventies. She looked at me and said, "I will never forget the day my ex-husband decided he wanted to end our marriage." She said at the time, she thought it was the worst thing that could have happened and that the pain was just awful. I could feel her pain. It was so real to me when we spoke. But then, she smiled and said, "But now I am happier than ever." I asked her if she remarried. She smiled an even bigger smile than before and said, "NO! Why should I remarry? I have a few boyfriends now and I live my life just the way I like living my life."

My goal in sharing her story with you is to let you know that divorce is really painful and hard, but she, along with myself and many other people, is proof positive, that after it is over, you truly can and will find happiness. I promise.

First There is Euphoria

Some people actually experience immediate happiness with their divorce. Often it's a temporary feeling of euphoria. Please make note: it goes away.

I have to share this story here. Just the other day I was getting my nails done when a very young woman sat next to me. She was so excited. She was getting a divorce! She wanted the entire salon to know about it, too. She told us how she was with her partner a total of seven years and married for three years. She was getting her nails done for her date that night. She had reconnected with an old friend on Facebook. What I found so interesting about this meeting was that as we spoke, I mentioned having time alone and how it's beneficial for everyone after a divorce. Her response was: "Yes, I agree. I am having the time of my life flirting and dating again."

Hmm...Perhaps we each had different definitions of what alone time is. I couldn't help but notice how all she could talk about was the fun she was having flirting again. It was clear she needed some external validation. And that's fine. We all do sometimes. We just need to be able to get that same kind of validation from inside ourselves, too, at some point.

She might be loving the flirting and the dating today, and maybe a month from today or more, but that euphoria will eventually die down. And that's okay, too. In fact, it's perfectly normal and needs to happen. And when the euphoria goes away, *that* will be the perfect time for her to begin thinking about what she truly wants from her new life.

Regardless, whether you experience a similar euphoria at being free or if you never do, you will need to stop and think for a little while. You will need to dig deep to figure out what you want your post-divorced life to be like. That will be your first step to attaining an authentically happy life, like my seventy-plus-year-old friend.

Dig Deep

After my second divorce, I went on an incredible life-changing journey of self discovery and self love that taught me how to bounce back from both divorces. I went to weekly counseling and worked hard on breaking through from the old person I was inside—the insecure, feeling unworthy little girl—to become a strong and happy adult.

We all need to do some serious soul searching and dig deep to get real with why our marriages did not last. If you don't get to the bottom of the situation, if you don't understand the differences, you will stay stuck and possibly even end up repeating the mistakes with another partner.

In chapter six, I present you with my four-step, Bounce Back Into You plan to help you get to the root of your issues regarding your divorce. It's not an easy gig. You'll need to be painfully, brutally honest about your role in the divorce—which is different from finding fault with yourself. For example, I realized one of the reasons my marriages didn't make it was the fact that I had no idea how to love, fight and make-up, and move on—you know, key elements for being able to stay committed to being committed to another person. On top of that, I had no idea what love was, and certainly didn't have any idea on *how* to love.

Those personal discoveries helped me realize I'd been living my life by going through the motions. Like many people, I had lived my life on a daily basis with my head down. I did what I needed to do to fulfill my role in the world, in my life, in my job. I didn't truly live. So when I dug deep, I not only figured out what happened in my marriages, but I also figured out who my real, authentic self was.

Heads Up!

When our heads are down, it's as if we are hiding from who we truly are, as if we're living by playing the same old tapes over and over again in our lives instead of actively living. Living with our heads down prevents us from finding happiness.

When you go on a journey of self-discovery, when you dig deep, you are forced to clean out your skeletons and face your demons head on. And when you discover you have the strength to do that, you also realize you have the strength to say: *Enough! I am not listening to those old tapes anymore. I am good enough. I am smart enough. I am enough, me and me alone.*

You already know the basics: divorce means you and your partner have decided you no longer want to be married and live in the same home. If you have children, it means the children now have two homes.

But can you get more specific? Ask yourself what your life really looks like in your new home. Are you happy there? Why are you not happy? What would make you happy? What do you need to work through to find that happiness?

Before you start asking those questions, though, I want to be sure you keep something in mind. If any of your answers begin with something like "I would be happy if my ex- . . ." Stop and think about what you're saying. These questions are for what *you* can do to help *you*. They are not about what or how your spouse can do for you. You can only control yourself. What do *you* need to work through to find happiness?

I promise you, you can bounce back and find your happily ever after–but first you need to get your head up and focus on you. I guarantee you it is possible. I never imagined I would be divorced twice. But today, I accept that my divorces were part of my journey to get me to here, to the joyful place I am today.

So think about your journey to this point and look at your role. Own your role. Personal responsibility is a must for you to begin a new life with a new improved version of you.

Be Your Own Best Friend

Recently, I met a woman who had been a stay-at-home mom, married for fifteen years, had two kids and never worked a day outside her home while she was married. Man, was she glowing when she told me her story! I shared with her that I was writing this book and her response to me was: "Oh my God! Please share with your readers that my life has never been better. Once I got focused on me, my life turned around!" In fact, she told me she would not be the person she was that day without having divorced. She was truly thankful it had happened.

That woman's positive attitude was infectious. She didn't let her divorce suck her dry of all the good she had to offer herself or her loved ones. In fact, she found the impetus she needed to be her own best friend because of her divorce. Regardless of how well you're supported (or not) by the people that you know, remember to be your own best friend. Be that person who reminds you, especially in the early days, to take good care of yourself.

Anytime we are faced with emotional upheaval, we need to take better care of ourselves than ever before. And few people will argue with the belief that divorce causes great emotional upheaval!

Think about what it means to be a best friend to yourself. What would your best friend do for you when you're feeling stressed or blue about your divorce? Well, your best friend would probably insist on doing things with you that you love to do. Your best friend would definitely make sure you found joy in your daily life. So, if you were your own best friend, what would you do for yourself? Make a list of those things and keep it on hand for anytime you feel like you need an emotional boost.

You don't have to come up with *big deal* things. It's true when people say the little things in life can have great meanings.

Here are five things I enjoy doing. I make sure I follow through on them when my life seems especially busy, extra emotional, or when it's just not going easily.

1. Spend more time alone. There is nothing better for the soul than some alone time to stop, think and evaluate where your life is and where you are going.
2. Spend time with loved ones. This is a great reminder of all the good you have in your life. It can be a close friend, a sister, or anyone who helps you feel better about being you. Let's face it: we cannot all be our own cheerleaders all the time. We do need to rely on others to help us get through the tough times. And, to me divorce was one hell of a tough time, both times.
3. Buy a ticket. Go to a show, or a movie or a sporting event – anything you love to do. Just do it. For me, I love going to shows on Broadway or to sporting events. Unfortunately, there were times when I simply did not have the money for the show or sports game, so I would pick a movie I wanted to see and go see it. A movie can take you to another world for a few hours. During a divorce, we need that away time.

23

4. Light candles. I love to work with a lit candle next to me. There is something about the glow that creates a beautiful sense. And the flickering light tends to make me breathe easier and smile. Whatever makes you smile, make sure the reminders are next to you on your desk or somewhere in the room you frequent most. I have pictures framed of me with my children in almost every room in the house. Whatever it takes to make you smile.
5. Me Time. Me time is different from alone time. Me Time is time spent at the gym, getting my nails done, listening to an inspirational talk. Me time is spent doing something that feels good for me. Alone time is time spent in quiet reflection about my life.

Nothing Lasts Forever

The initial stages of a divorce can seem so daunting and life changing that it feels like the situation will feel horrible forever. Let me remind you now, and then you must remind yourself often: this is all temporary.

As my mom would always say: "This, too, shall pass."

UGH! I hated that phrase! Every time I would call her with some news about my divorce, she would say those magic words: *this, too, shall pass*. Those four words are so annoying–but so true. I promise you, you will not live in a limbo world for forever. One day your divorce will be final. And one day you will be happily divorced.

When I think back to both my divorces, what stands out most is how drained I was from worrying about it all and thinking *Oh my God! This will never end*. There were so many times when I thought everything was done, like when we'd finish the property settlement agreement, and that I could relax and move on, only to discover there was yet something else that needed my time and energy.

But time and energy are nothing compared to the emotional toil. So when I say it will be over, that *that, too, will pass,* let me make an amendment to it so you're not set up for false expectations. The nuts and bolts of the agreement, the legalities of it all, will pass much more quickly than the emotional piece. That part can last a long time and, instead of having a finite life span based on a calendar or how quickly people can sign their name, the emotional piece can last indefinitely. It's up to you how long the emotional upheaval impacts you.

A key point to remember: the emotional upheaval doesn't have to last long at all. And really, the way to shorten it is to take charge of your emotions and keep them out of the process as much as possible.

Sounds impossible, I know. But it's not. I'll discuss what I mean in the next chapter.

Chapter 4:
Removing the Emotion

Let's Be Honest, It's an Emotional Time

While everyone agrees that divorce is an emotionally charged time, I don't think anyone really understands just how emotionally charged until he or she is experiencing it. I remember getting into conversations with my ex-spouses and getting so worked up that it impacted everything about me for the rest of the day, or maybe even the week. It literally made me feel depleted. I think my second divorce made me feel worse than the first. There I was in my forties. Divorced twice and I had no money. And when I say no money, I mean *NO* money, so I was empty emotionally and financially.

I ended the last chapter talking about how the emotional upheaval doesn't have to last long. It really is up to you to decide how long it will last. And you make that decision by being willing to let go of the anger and the hurt, to stop wanting revenge or to one-up your ex-. That might sound impossible, but I suggest you try it bit by bit, one emotion at a time. Here are a few ideas to think on to help you.

Stuff

We all want what we want–right? But when you begin the whole process of divvying your money and home goods, it's hard to remember they are just things and not parts of us. The table that has sentimental value to you because it has been in your family for generations should be yours. I get that. And probably, most ex-spouses will get that, too. But, what about the things you bought together as a married couple? As you divide them, you need to do more. You need to stop and think about what possessions are really yours versus his, and you also need to figure out what is really worth spending time arguing about.

Sometimes, if you're honest with yourself, you'll realize that you are not truly attached to a particular item but that by claiming you are, you'll make your ex-'s life harder. Trust me: don't go there. In the end, you'll just make your life harder. Think about that.

Try to remove the desire to hurt your ex-. No matter how badly you feel he or she deserves it, clinging to the need to hurt, or get even, will only keep *you* feeling hurt and angry. Is anything really worth keeping you stuck in such negativity?

I can't stress enough how important it is to control and remove the emotion from the nuts and bolts of your divorce. I didn't do it with my first divorce and it hurt everyone involved. Most importantly, it hurt my son.

Move and Make it YOURS!

Sometimes you are forced to lose your home when you lose your spouse. An entire house, a home, can seem like something that's too personal or important to handle without emotion. But it doesn't have to be. Maybe all that's required is that you achieve a different perspective.

During my first marriage, I lived in a single home with a pool on a nice sized lot of land. I went from that home, one with a lovely master bedroom, beautiful views and decorated just the way I wanted, to a tiny townhouse—a rented, tiny townhouse packed on a street of other tiny townhouses like sardines in a can.

But, guess what? I loved my tiny townhouse because it was mine! I will never forget the many nights laying in my bed in my new house and thinking I loved the brown curtains (they were the ugliest brown curtains I had ever seen, but they were *mine* and they came with *my* house!) The house had ugly gray carpet throughout, white walls and tile in the bathrooms from the 1960s. None of that mattered. All that mattered was that it was my new house and I loved it! Why? Because I had finally found peace. After living in a stressful world, my new home was perfect for me.

The day I moved, I went and spent my last amount of money on a new couch and love seat set, complete with two end tables and a coffee table. I thought, and I still do, that it was the prettiest set ever. Why? Because *I* bought it and it was in *my* newly rented townhouse. My advice to you is to appreciate your new house, apartment or whatever your new home is—

even if you are living with family. Appreciate the peace of mind you have and do not take that for granted. If you curse and lament it and wish you were back in your old, beautiful home, you will never find the peace you need to heal from your divorce.

Your Ex- Has Feelings, Too–Even If the Divorce Is Your Spouse's Idea

Perhaps the hardest time to keep your emotions from taking control is when you think about your ex-spouse's emotions. Regardless of whose idea it is to get a divorce, you must always remember, your ex- has feelings, too.

I know that some people feel justified in using their divorce as an opportunity to get back at their spouses. I have heard some of the worst stories. One man told me his ex-wife promised she would ruin him financially and personally. She continues to this day to make his life much harder than it has to be. There are spouses out there who truly find pleasure in hurting not just their ex-partner, but also their children through manipulation. I will never ever understand why people want to make their children be pawns in the middle of their game–the game of getting even.

Why do they do this? I am sure they are thinking along the lines of *because he hurt me* or *because she deserves this.* I just can't agree with that non-logic. That sounds to me like those folks are stuck in their initial emotions.

I guess you can say when it comes to divorce, I am a realist. Look, I get it. You thought you could work through the differences, you tried and didn't succeed. Maybe you even believe the whole divorce is the other person's fault. But remember: divorce is just one way for a marriage to end. It's when differences are too great to overcome. How can you justify ruining another human being's life because two people couldn't work out their differences?

The process of divorce is not fun, but there can be a wonderful life after divorce. It's your job to create that wonderful life and live it. Going through a divorce—with all the meetings with your attorney, with the time and effort needed to gather financial information, and the craziness involved in creating a schedule of visitation for the children—it becomes a temporary, part-time job. If you put energy and time into making "someone pay" on top of that part-time job you'll have little, if anything, left to experience joy in your life. <u>I urge you not to get stuck in revenge.</u> When your intent is revenge, you will not be able to heal yourself. You need to heal so you can grow and move on to the brightest possible future.

Your Ex- Has Feelings, Too–Even If the Divorce Is *Your* Idea

Imagine this: it's a typical day. You wake up, go to work, come home. At some point in your normal evening, your spouse turns to you and says, "I want a divorce." It's a life-changing moment for both people, right?

Right. Well, that's where I went wrong with my divorces, and I think many of us do. We think, *I want a divorce.* The reasons for it are so very clear in our own minds that we just don't understand why it is so hard for the other person to get it. We simply think: *this will be great. I'll get divorced and then I'll be free.*

If those or similar thoughts are going through your head, STOP! Please, please stop. Take a moment to separate yourself from your emotions and remember you once loved this person. You share a life together. And now you are changing not just *your* life but someone else's. Your spouse might be blindsided and devastated.

I was the one who wanted both my divorces. I can honestly say I am not proud of how I handled either one. I was so excited. I was like a child who was given a free pass to a theme park. I loved the adventure. I was dating within weeks of separating. Thank God they did not have Facebook when I was first divorced!

I never took the time to look back and mourn for both of us, to remember that I once loved that person. Divorce is an end to something that was once very special to both partners. I think we owe it to each other, and to our children if we have them, to try our hardest to stop, think and respect our spouse's feelings. In chapter seven I go into great detail about dating, but I want to get this one bit of advice in here now: if you are dating someone right away, at least wait until everyone involved can get used to the idea of the divorce before you start broadcasting it. There is really no need to flaunt your new partner around and there is really no need to introduce them to your children.

The golden rule of divorce should always be – kids first! And to that end, in the next chapter we talk about some healthy ways to help your children through the divorce. But first, a helpful exercise.

An Exercise to Think More Positively About Your Ex-

You can, and should, try to remember that your ex-partner is still the partner you once chose to marry and now have a child with. Treating your spouse with respect, even if only for the sake of your children, might seem like an impossible task. However, I have an excellent exercise for you to do. Indulge me, please. After you do this exercise, keep the results near you at all times. Use them to defuse any negative emotions that might arise when you are dealing with your former spouse.

1. Take a plain piece of paper and write down five (yes, five) reasons you married your ex- in the first place.
2. Now, write down five positive qualities that your child or children share with your ex-.

See that? Now, you have ten positive things to think about regarding your ex-. You now have what we can refer to as the *Positive Ex-* sheet. So, when you are angry, and want to tell your ex- off, stop, breathe and review the Positive Ex- sheet. You ask why?

By reading the Positive Ex- sheet, you will remind yourself that your ex- was not always bad. That you once deemed this person worthy of marrying. And although the marriage didn't work, it wasn't all bad—you have the proof in your hand. Then remind yourself if you stay focused on the bad in the your past, you will not be able to move on to the good in your future.

If you do not have children, you can still write the list of five top qualities you loved about your ex-.

Use the list as your go-to when you are angry. Use it to defuse your resentment. Use it each time before you call your attorney.

Whatever you do, please do not, I repeat *do not,* make rash decisions about your divorce agreement without thought and contemplation with your divorce attorney. Remember, you are paying them to help make sure your divorce is fair. If you call your attorney hysterical crying, which I have done, or screaming, which I have also done, you are wasting money and emotion. If you call them and say, "my ex- wants this, and after much thought I have decided to do that," you will save yourself time, money and energy.

Looking back–Special Notes to My Exes

I keep in touch with both my ex-husbands, but I don't think I've ever really told them how I feel about our marriages. I'm not even sure they know I wish I had handled them differently. To help remedy that, I thought I'd write letters to them both to expresses a little of my gratitude and appreciation for our time together.

Dear Joe,

> *As part of my second book, about bouncing back from divorce, I thought I would write a letter to you since you have done a great job of bouncing back; and I know it has not been easy for you.*
>
> *I am thrilled for your happiness with your fiancée Kathy and her family.*
>
> *I know we had our tough years in the beginning. We were both so emotional and explosive at times with our actions and our words. Our marriage had lots of good, and some really bad. I want you to know that when I look back at our life together, I do remember the happy and fun times, and I often tell Jacob about them, so he understands that at one time we loved each other very much.*
>
> *I know that without us, there would be no Jacob and I might never have known the beauty of unconditional love, because the day I delivered Jacob I fell in love with being a mom – forever. Now our son, Jacob, is 20 years-old and what a wonderful person he is. Jacob is blessed with having you and your family in his life.*
>
> *My wish for you is that you and Kathy continue to be as happy as you are today.*
>
> *My wish for us for the next 40 or so years, maybe more, is that we can be friends for Jacob. We can both sit next to each other and celebrate at his college graduation and share so many wonderful memories that he has in store, whatever they are. He*

deserves to have both of us, his mom and his dad supporting him, knowing that no matter what happens in life he can always count on his parents.

My wish for Jacob is that for the remainder of his life he knows that both his parents love him and support him, and will always be there for him.

This year at your mom's funeral might have been the first time we have spoken to each other with genuine respect and

admiration. Today, I write this letter to you and hope that it was not the last time we are cordial and kind to each other, we owe it to ourselves and to Jacob.

My wish is that together we continue to celebrate Jacob and all of the joy he brings to all the lives he touches and always remind him how truly loved he is by both of our families.

With deepest sincerity –
Lisa

Dear Richard,

I love that you are still a part of my family.

I love that you continue to attend holiday dinners for so many reasons. I know it means the world to Ari and my family.

How funny was it that the other night you and I were joking after the holiday dinner that one day when you remarry, I will be your "best ex-wife?"

It is so incredible to me that you and I are such good friends; maybe I should restate that, I mean that after all we have been through we are still great friends, and truly have mutual love and respect for each other.

When we talk about our past, which we rarely rehash, we both smile, and laugh because we started out as friends and joke that we should have stayed friends. But, we know if we had, we would never have our own personal piece of happiness and sunshine: Ari!

I still laugh inside when I think about our few trips to marriage counseling and the counselor asked us what we were missing and we both responded with – chemistry. She replied, well if you did not have chemistry when you were first married, what makes you think six years later you should have it? When I try to explain to people what our relationship is like today, I say this, "today he is like a very close brother."

Thank you for always supporting me through good times and bad. I love that I can share a bad day with you and you never judge; you just listen. I love that I can count on you to celebrate all the good life has to offer all of us, Jacob, Ari and me. Your texts are always one of the first to say a kind word when you think I need to hear one. Your mom once said to me, "my son is a kind soul." Guess what? She was not kidding. You are truly a kind person and you have instilled that into Ari and Jacob.

Thank you for always being so kind, patient and generous to Ari, Jacob and me. There is no doubt that you love all of us and will always be there for us.

Thank you for always being my friend.

As your friend, my wish for you is that one day you will not have to work so hard. You are one of the hardest working people I have ever met. And, if there is anyone I know who can enjoy life, it is you.

My wish for you is to find the woman you can have it all with: the friendship we share with the added bonus of chemistry. Chemistry so great that when you two walk in the room it can be felt by all to envy. You deserve nothing less, my friend.

My wish for you is to live a long and healthy life so you can continue to fly, play the drums with Ari, and one day, dance at our son's wedding, and Jacob's too.

My wish for you is find complete joy and happiness with Ari, Jacob, me and one day, your special someone surrounding you for the rest of your life.

With all my love and respect for my friend, and partner in raising Ari.

Love always,

Lisa

Chapter 5:
Co-Parenting after Divorce
You are Life Partners in Raising Children

Co-Parenting Is the Best

This is the chapter where you really get to meet Richard, my second ex-husband. He is a great partner in raising our son, Ari. He has always been involved and an active participant throughout his life. Together, we figured out a way to co-parent Ari, so that we are all happy with our relationship and Ari is blossoming as our son.

But, before we get on to co-parenting, I want to share a few tidbits about what I've learned when it comes to helping your children deal with the divorce.

Don't Keep It a Secret—They Already Know!

When you decide you want the divorce, please do not keep it a secret from your children, especially the older children who "get it" way sooner than you think. I remember when I went to tell my older son, Jacob, that I was divorcing my second husband. His response was something like: "why did you wait so long?" He knew already, just by watching our behaviors and actions. Looking back, we both should have told him and Ari a lot sooner than we did.

A Word of Warning—Children Watch and Learn

Don't wait to start figuring out what's best for your children. From the very beginning, what's best for them is that you be the parent your children *deserve*. Always remember to show them *with your actions and behavior* how imperative it is to have respect and compassion for their other parent. Remember this—your ex- is still your child's mom or dad. That will never change. It's up to *you* to be a role model and raise the bar in parental excellence.

Remember our children watch what we do. We are their greatest teachers. Show your children how to love and be loved. Every time you are about to say something negative, remind yourself that you are setting an example and teaching your children how to behave. Do not make your children feel guilty for being with your ex-, or worse, yet don't make them feel guilty for liking your ex-'s new partner. Similarly, do not make your children feel guilty for inheriting traits of their parents. Children do not choose their parents. They cannot help being like their fathers or mothers. Guilt and shame will only have a negative impact on your children that they don't deserve. They deserve the best possible parents—parents who love them regardless of how much they are like the ex-spouse!

Your children should be the primary reason why you do not use divorce as a tool to punish your spouse. We all question why there is so much anger and bullying in our society. Children often learn what they live. The lesson we should teach our children about divorce is not hatred, not revenge, but how to bounce back from things ending. Teach them how to end relationships with grace and dignity. Teach them that when someone does not want to be married anymore–yes, it stinks and it's painful and it takes time to get over the pain—but we do not need to make our spouse and our children pay a very dear price.

Create a New Normal

Another thing you shouldn't wait long to do is figure out a new normal. You need to make sure your children feel secure and stable as soon as possible. A normal routine will offer your children a sense of security

So what do I mean by normal? Normal is whatever you want it to be for you and your family. One good idea is to remember the fun things from before your divorce and try to stick with them. If you had ice-cream and pizza every Friday night, then continue to do that for the children. During a divorce is probably one of the most important times for you to ensure your children get the stability and sense of security that they need.

My Personal Parental Divorce Tips:

Always remember your children will have their own emotional journey with your divorce. And even though they may be mature or seem like they can handle it (or even want the divorce), the following are a few things to keep in mind to help them not only deal with the hurdles, but maybe even not notice them:

- Extra TLC is needed more than ever. Hugs and kisses and lots of *I love you*. *Mommy loves you*, *Daddy loves you*. Children need extra reminders during this critical time in their lives, after all, if it seems like Mommy and Daddy don't love each other anymore, a small child might worry that Mommy and Daddy might stop loving him or her.
- Always be honest and never hide the truth from your children. They deserve the truth and it will prevent them from being angry at you later when they discover it by accident.
- Tell the school. The guidance office is a great resource for your children.
- Remind your children frequently that the divorce is not because of them, that it has nothing to do with them.
- Keep the traditions alive, whatever they are. Keep them going for the children. If your traditions need to change, involve the children in the conversation.
- Family therapy is key! Make the investment in seeking a professional to help you and your family through this challenging time.
- Family meetings are a great way to communicate what changes are happening. And they can simply be a safe place where children can ask questions, have a voice and be involved.
- Family night spent playing games, watching movies, whatever. Make nights dedicated to the family. Remind your children that they are part of a family, even if one of their parents does not live at home.

The Fun Parent

I think it is really important to remember that we cannot make up for the divorce. We cannot buy our children toys and/or anything else to make the pain go away.

My first ex- used to drive me nuts with those kinds of behaviors. My son Jacob would come home from seeing his dad with a new this or a new that. I would get so upset because I wanted Jacob to think of his dad as his dad, not as someone who would give him a new toy every time he saw him. I was working to make sure he had three meals, did his homework and brushed his teeth, and then there was his dad: the "fun" parent.

News flash: that status goes away. As the children grow up, they begin to understand the difference. And they learn to appreciate the parent who shows them stability and unconditional love.

A close friend of mine, who had recently divorced, once spoke to me at the end of my son's birthday party. She said, "I don't know what to do with the boys for the rest of the day." I told her to do exactly what they did before the divorce. She was concerned because their dad was the "fun" parent. I looked at her and assured her that her boys needed consistency, that they needed to know how to be home with their mom, and that they needed to create their own version of what is normal for them. It didn't matter if their dad was training them for the fun Olympics. Those games didn't exist. She needed to prepare her children for real life with chores, responsibilities, rules and consequences.

Parenting Pledge

I think everyone MUST stop putting children in the middle of divorce. There is never a good enough reason to justify doing it. It only results in inflicting damage on the most innocent bystanders. Your divorce is not about the children; it is about two adults who get married, then decide they no longer love each other and want a divorce, right?

I know it's not simple. There is a lot of pain and sadness involved. But when you put your kids dead center in the middle of the fighting and discomfort, you only worsen their pain and sadness.

I truly wish everyone, and I do mean everyone, who decides to get a divorce had to take a Parenting Pledge, which had to be signed and filed with the courts along with the petition for divorce. The pledge would include guidelines for behavior while going through a divorce. For example, do not fight in front of the children. I remember one day, I was livid with my second ex-husband and we were fighting on the phone, I turned around and there was our son, Ari, standing in the room. He knew I was fighting with, let's be clear, screaming at his dad. After seeing the look on his face, I made a promise to myself to never allow that to happen again. It was heartbreaking.

I wish I could say that I have not witnessed people putting their children in the middle. But that simply is not the case. I understand going through a divorce is one of the most emotionally charged times of your life. But it's not just about you.

I know there will be people reading this saying: "Is she crazy? Remove the emotion? My ex- did x, y and z to me!"

Trust me, I get that! But no matter what the reason, if we all try to step back, think it through and pretend we are giving advice to our friends about how they can handle a dilemma while fighting for alimony, maybe, just maybe, we can make our decisions from a place of *what is best for the family?* Yes, you are still a family. Your child, or children, was born out of the love you once shared with your spouse. If you have children with your ex-spouse, you will be "connected family" for the rest of your lives. I know it is hard to grasp the concept.

One thing that will quickly become apparent after your divorce is that you were wrong if you thought once the divorce was finalized you'd have nothing to do with your ex-.If you have a child with that person, you will be enmeshed in each other's lives for the rest of your life—'til death do you part!

The good news is you get to set the rules on how that will work. And it's all your choice—just like anything in life. This is your time to decide what you want the next chapter of your life to look like, your life as a post-divorce parent. Notice I didn't say "single parent"?

And Now About Co-Parenting

It is possible to have an excellent relationship with your ex- and provide a truly loving and supportive two-household family for your children. I know it's possible because that's what I do with Richard.

It didn't start that way immediately. I would say our co-parenting ebbed and flowed in the beginning until everyone settled in with their new lives.

> **I decided my ideal relationship with both of my boys is to love them, guide them and help them make the best possible choices so they can flourish throughout their adult life.**

To make it easier, I suggest you sit down and think about what roles you want both you and your ex- to take in your child's life. Ask: how did you and your ex- parent before the divorce? Does that need to be changed or enhanced? I truly believe that we always need to ask ourselves, *what is best for the kids*? Please only think about what YOU want to be to your child, not what you think your ex-should be. Remember, you can only control yourself.

Remember when I spoke about removing the emotion from your divorce? If you do it nowhere else in your divorce, at least do it when it comes to co-parenting! They always say you learn from your mistakes, and I freely admit with Jacob's father it was virtually impossible to co-parent. I learned plenty from those mistakes. We tried, but there was so much emotion and bitterness it was always a battle, a battle of who could win the argument at hand.

Looking back I realize it was pointless. The only person who suffered from our battles was our son. My belief is that when children witness their parents battling over every little thing, they realize quickly they need to stop the insanity. So, what do they do? They attempt to make it easy on their parents. They agree with whichever they are with them and you can only imagine what happens next. Always remember, it's your job as an adult to make it easier on the children when it comes to divorce, not the other way around.

Co-Parenting From the Other Perspective
When I asked Richard if he would like to contribute to my book the answer was *YES!* Here is what co-parenting means to Richard:

> My situation of parenting my son, Ari, is one of co-parenting with his mother, the author of this book. Succeeding at co-parenting means **COOPERATING** from the beginning. Co-parenting means moving aside the adversarial relationship between two parents and taking that negative energy to a new positive level...then investing the positive emotion into co-parenting. It's clearly respecting each other, communicating what you both want for your child and respecting each other, despite any differences you may have had in the past. Focus on the child's growth and well-being as you work out the details together.

So What Exactly Does It Mean to Co-Parent?

Co-parenting has many responsibilities attached to it, including being involved with your child's extracurricular activities and schoolwork. It means disciplining, praising, teaching and above all, both parents showing the child they equally love him or her. Putting the past behind and planning the future is the key to successful co-parenting.

Here are some steps and best practices that Richard and I try to commit too. Notice, I said "try." It's not always easy because no two situations are identical. For example, right now, as I am writing this book, Richard is working an excessive amount of hours so Ari spends 95% of his time with me. In a perfect world, Ari would see his dad every other weekend and one day during the week according to the courts. But here is the problem: the courts do not live in our houses with our schedules and everyone needs to remember to practice flexibility. Flexibility is a critical component to life.

We will discuss it with your dad

I do think one of the best practices we have in our family, is we never make any major decision without including Ari's dad. This is how I see it: if we made decisions together before we were divorced, why not continue with that practice? And, not only does it work, but it sends a message to our son that we are both a part of his life and we are both involved in making family decisions for his well being.

Finances

We never let finances get in the way. Nor do we discuss money in front of our son. And also, we do not decide to split expenses for one particular item over another. We agreed a long time ago that we would split most expenses and that is why child support is in place. I made a personal commitment to myself a long time ago that I would never allow my children to feel like monetary burdens or that they were somehow a large ticket item. There are people who will say things like, *my kids cost me too much money*, or *I am nothing more than the bill payer to my kids and that breaks my heart.* Yes, children are expensive, but they are whether you are married or divorced, right?

I remember when I was in high school I had a dear friend who was in the middle of her parents' divorce. It was so painful to watch. I will never forget when it was time for our senior prom. Her parents fought over every cent she needed, she even joked that her parents were fighting over prom shoes. She cried to me because she said, "my parents got divorced and my life will never be the same." It's true, we, I am speaking about the adults who get divorced, need to remember the children did not ask for it. It is hard on everyone, especially the children.

Traditions, Birthday Parties and More

Here is a pet peeve of mine: when the parents cannot get along well enough to help celebrate the children's special events. It really makes me sad when I hear people talk about having two birthday parties or two graduation parties. Whatever the celebration, my wish is we all try to get along for the kids' sake.

Imagine being a child and your parents just got separated or divorced and now you cannot have the entire family in one room to celebrate *you*. The message we send to our children is that we cannot suck it up and get along for *them,* the kids that matter the most.

Discipline: Time to Back Each Other

Another big, big thing to me is that everyone agrees on the rules, expectations and punishments. One time I was so mad at Ari, I called Richard and said "I need your help." Ari was being stubborn. He did not want to go to baseball practice and no matter what I said, he was not budging. I could not take it anymore. It was a stressful day and I needed some backing. I called Richard and told him the situation. He calmly said, "Put him on the phone." Ari spoke to his dad for a few minutes, and then we hung up, got dressed and went to practice. I thanked Richard and that was that. Kids will push our buttons and test the limits. We need to teach our children that no matter what happens, we the adults, are united, we stand together and are and in charge.

Extended Family

I also think it is important to remind you that the extended family stays family even after the divorce and that is the way it truly should be. If there was a close family relationship before the divorce, there is no reason for that to stop. After all, you are not divorcing the entire family, just the ex-.

Both my sons have relationships with their extended families and I love that. In fact, when my first ex-mother-in-law died, I went to the funeral and was welcomed as a member of the family. We need to teach our children the value of family, how much they can learn from their grandparents, and that extended family is a blessing.

Extended family is like having an entire cheerleading squad and offensive line for your kids who are their own quarterbacks in life. I had to throw that in. I love football and it's a really good analogy. Your children need more than just mom or dad. They need both parents and then some. Let's face it, raising children is not an easy job, so don't make it harder on yourself by taking away or cutting people out of your children's lives because you got divorced. In fact, I love that my family and some of my close friends are close to my children so they can support and love them as they grow and become adults.

Chapter 6:
How to Bounce Back from Divorce

Finding Happiness—It's Waiting for You
Right now, stop and take a figurative look around. Pick out a friend or two who might have gone through a divorce and see that their life is just fine, probably even better than it was before. Pain from a divorce does not need to equal a lifetime of self-inflicted punishment. As you read through my book, please remind yourself that life happens, divorce happens, and you can and will bounce back.

Bounce Back into YOU!
My four-step Bounce Back Into You plan in my original book, LIFE HAPPENS: BOUNCE BACK! has been adapted to fit a divorce situation. The plan below walks you through the basic steps, then after the plan I use a real-life example from my own experience to help you along the way.

Step 1: Get Clarity–Get to the real, emotional root of your divorce.

Getting clarity with your divorce means you get to the root issues, the true causes of your divorce. It means you discover what underlying emotional or physical needs were not being met in your marriage, what philosophical or lifestyle differences you and your spouse were unable to overcome, and the true nature of the expectations you had when you got married to begin with.

Step one, when done thoroughly, will help identify what areas you personally need to focus on in order to heal from the pain of your divorce. It will also show you where you can grow and make your life better because of the situation.

Here's an exercise to help you get started on getting clarity:
- List all the reasons for the divorce. Be brutally honest and include everything, including minute details like *I just couldn't take him leaving a wet towel on the bed one more time.*
- Now, try to name the feelings associated with each of those issues; write them down.
- Do you see a pattern? Is "anger" associated with most of those reasons? A sense of unfairness? Frustration? A little of everything?
- Review the list again, ask yourself *why* you think each one happened, and write down your answers. Again, be brutally honest. If you said *we just grew apart*, ask why you think that happened? Was it that neither of you were interested in what the other was doing? Was one person busier than the other, so the other had to find new interests? Be sure to ask *why* with each of the answers, including those for the minute details. Why did you get upset with him leaving the wet towel on the bed? Was it you saw it as laziness, hence a weakness in him that you resented? Did you feel disrespected because he is mature enough to handle the laundry, but he left it to you as if you were his personal maid? Get to all the issues.
- Again, name the emotions you feel regarding each reason why.
- Once again, do you see a pattern? Do you see repeated emotions from both lists?
- Note the primary emotions. Those emotions are the root cause of your divorce.

Step 2: Get Real.

As I mentioned just few lines above, knowing which emotions are underlying your marital problems is key in identifying where and how you need to heal and grow from your divorce. In order to start doing just that, you have to do step two and **Get Real** with the situation. That is, look at those lists of emotions and ask yourself what your responsibility is for each of them.

For example, if anger is dominant, you'll need to understand where that anger came from. Usually we become angry because our expectations are not being met. So if anger is your primary emotion, ask yourself:
- What were your expectations regarding each of the reasons you listed in step one for your marriage falling apart?

- Did you ever clearly express those expectations or did you assume he/she knew them?
- How realistic were those expectations? As always, be honest! Yes, a grown man should be able to throw a wet towel in a hamper; that would be a realistic expectation. However, if he never realized it left a wet splotch on your side or that it angered you, it's your fault that you let it happen without being up front about how it made you feel. Did you resent being a football widow? If so, did you know going into your marriage that he was paralyzed in front of a TV every Sunday during the fall and winter? If that answer is *yes,* then expecting him to automatically stop watching football just because he married you, is unrealistic.
- As you look over those questions, do you see how you need to change the way you express yourself or what you expect from others in order to be happy?

Ask yourself similar questions for each of the dominant emotions that stood out in step one.

- If resentment stands out, that suggests you feel you were treated unfairly, judged wrongly, or felt put upon.
- Feelings of insecurity often mean you were expecting other people to determine your value and to make you feel worthy, instead of relying on yourself to do that.
- Fear suggests that you knew you were in an unhealthy relationship with no options, so you'll need to examine how you got there.

Now, comes a biggie: as you narrow down the feelings connected to your role in the divorce, can you think back over your life to when you've felt those feelings before? Is the divorce part of a pattern of your behaviors, choices or beliefs that you've established throughout your life?

Understanding and getting to the truth behind why your marriage failed can be a tricky exercise. You could easily say *he cheated*, or *she was dishonest*, and wash your hands of it. But if you do that, you will never heal. You will not grow with such surface answers.

Your goal must be to dig a little deeper and ask things like *Why did he cheat?* Or *Why was she dishonest?* And keep digging deeper and deeper until you feel like you can't dig any further to discover the real reason it happened.

Step 3: Get a Vision

Steps one and two should have brought to light areas about yourself you can focus on in order to change and grow, so that you can have a happier life and even happier relationships. But, to make sure you're heading in the right direction, you need to stop and think about what a happy life and happy relationships look like to you. That is, you need to figure out what it means to be content with your post-divorce life.

Look back over the patterns and insights you discovered in steps one and two and think on those emotions and causes and what you need to do to change them or overcome them:

- If anger was at the root, how can you change your expectations and still be happy? That is, what is really important to you in a relationship and what's not? Also, do you need to work on developing the inner strength necessary to communicate your expectations?
- Resentment could mean you need to examine who you are making responsible for your feelings. Remember that's always your responsibility, never another person's. So if resentment is your big issue, then you'll need to create a vision for yourself where you value you enough to stand up for yourself and not rely on other people to meet your needs.
- Insecurity suggests you need to create a vision focused on doing personal growth work to find your self-worth and self-confidence.

Ultimately, getting a vision means that you get real and take responsibility for your emotions, for why you feel the way you do, and then you create an idea, a vision, of how your life would look after you learn to master your emotions.

Getting a vision is really an exciting part of the process because it is when you really define what kind of life you want, post-divorce. You get to ask yourself *What's next?* Knowing there are no limits or boundaries. You get to decide what it is you need to do and will do in order to be the happy, healthy person you always wanted to be.

Step 4: Get a Plan

Now that you identified what you need to change and what you want your life to look like, it's time to make a plan. It's time to create and have the life you want and deserve.

Sometimes knowing what you want to change is all you need in order to make the change. Other times you need a little help. When it comes to changing your overall mindset in order to develop self-esteem, courage, or habitual thought patterns, there are a variety of tools and techniques you can try. I have a whole host of exercises in my first book, LIFE HAPPENS: BOUNCE BACK!, that can help. Among them:

- Create a vision board. This exercise is fun! Picture what you want your life to look like after the divorce is final. Take a big poster and draw a circle. In the center of the circle write your name. Now, like a pizza, divide it up into as many slices of life you want. Career, spirituality, relationships with family, friends, dating, finances. In the middle of each slice write a goal for it. For example: under family, your goal could be to spend more quality time with your children.

- Use Post It! Notes: write positive, supportive statements on Post It! Notes and stick them in places where you'll frequently seem them: bathroom mirror, coffee pot, dashboard, etc. Can't think of anything positive? How about: *I am stronger than I think. I am open to positive change. I am lovable and loving. I am perfectly me.*

- Develop personal mantras: similar to the Post It! Notes, devise a phrase or find a quote that you find soothing and inspirational. Memorize it and repeat it anytime you feel anxiety or stress. Repeat it as you walk from the copy room to your desk at work. Repeat it as you wait for the light to change from red to green in traffic.

- Enlist the help of friends or a support group. Never underestimate the power of a good group. You don't have to go it alone. Rally friends. Find a support group and if you can't find one that meets regularly, ask everyone you know who is divorced if they'd like to form one with you.

- Therapy, if none of the above is working give therapy a try. Therapy is NEVER a sign of weakness. It's a sign of strength to know when you need more and then to reach out and ask for it.

After my second divorce, I had to get real with why my marriages did not work. I took three years off from dating and had the greatest love affair of all: with myself. Those years helped me get clear about *why* my marriages failed and ultimately led to the development of my Bounce Back philosophy.

I asked myself a lot of tough questions, similar to what I'm asking you to do here. Clarity came for me after I identified what was really bothering me, what was really not working in a variety of situations and *my* role in each one.

My Life as Example

Here are a few examples that I hope will explain how to walk through the steps based on my first and second divorces. There were more reasons, but because the underlying emotional causes wound up being the same as the two I use below, for the sake of brevity I kept it to just two.

Step one: I found clarity

The first reason: *His hobbies drove me nuts!* That's what I told myself anyway. I blamed his hobbies as one of the reasons why our marriage failed. It was his fault: my first ex-husband had several hobbies that kept him away from the house and left me alone, feeling like I was not his priority, but that his hobbies were.

When I took the time to get to the root of my emotions, I realized I needed *him* to make me his priority because in my mind, if he showed me I was his priority, then that meant I was important, that I had value. In other words, one of the emotions ruling our marriage from my side, was my feelings of insecurity and not being good enough.

The second reason: both of my marriages were awful when it came to dealing with money. Both my ex-husbands and myself liked to enjoy life and spend money. We were always over spending. WE, not just them. I am not blaming anyone.

I really had to ask myself, *why were both of my marriages so undisciplined when it came to money? Why was there never enough? What were we doing wrong?* I also looked at motivation. *Why didn't I know what was coming in and out? Why did I turn a blind eye to my finances once I was married?*

I realized none of us wanted to be responsible for fear of having to tell the other person, "no." We didn't want to disappoint each other. We wanted the other to have whatever made them happy. And what was at the root of that? For me, it was the same ol' same ol': I feared I wasn't good enough as a person so I couldn't say "no" or he might not love me anymore.

Yuck.

Step 2: Getting Real

It wasn't the greatest feeling in the world to discover the real reasons why my marriages failed were because I was insecure, lacked confidence and just didn't feel good enough to be loved and accepted. But I plunged on anyway, to get real with the situation to see how I was responsible for my side of our relationships.

I dug deeper and realized that because I was insecure and unconfident, I was making it *his* job to show me I was important. And it wasn't. It's no one's job to do that but myself.

In my mind, my first husband was leaving me to do something better than spending time with me. Being with his friends meant he was having fun without me and since we were a married couple after all, weren't we supposed to spend all of our time together?

At that time in my life, I was looking for my husband to show me I was the most important thing to him by spending all his spare time with me. I didn't stop to think that he had friends and hobbies before we married and that he would want to continue those relationships after our marriage. I didn't stop to think that his time with friends and hobbies allowed me time to do the same and that if I valued myself I would make sure I had fun, too. And if I did that, then we could spend the time we did have together more happily and comfortably, then our conversations would be more enjoyable, we'd both be happier because we had fuller lives. I, at least, should have communicated that I wanted more time with him and what that *more time* meant to me. We all need relationship coaches and I think we would all benefit from some school, or a seminar or two, on how to communicate with your spouse. It all sounds so simple, but if it were, then why do so many marriages end in divorce?

Regarding, my finances, I went on to ask myself more questions. First, I took responsibility for my actions by asking things like: *What did I do to contribute to our spending?* Realizing I was spending just as much as he was, meant I had to take action with myself and get in control.

I also had to look at that *not good enough* belief mentality to realize it was truly my feelings of inadequacy, my insecurity that led me down the path of bad money habits. I knew I'd never be good with money until I valued myself to know I that I could say "no" and still be loved. I also knew I'd never be good with money until I was confident in my ability to handle it.

Step 3: My Vision

I knew I needed to change and evaluate what I wanted for me from a partner. I also needed to figure out how to value me in a relationship so that I could set fair and reasonable expectations on another person.

I realized that I, too, needed to have alone time, as well as time to spend with friends, if I was going to be a happy person. I couldn't make one person be my everything. It wasn't healthy nor was it realistic. I also realized the same would be true for my partner. So the vision I created included hobbies for me to pursue, deliberate attempts to reach out to more friends and still balance my time with a man who was equally active. In that vision, I see my relationship as one where my partner and I show our love for each other in the way we treat each other.

It was never realistic for me to ask my ex-husband to quit his hobbies. It would have been realistic for me to ask him to spend more time with me and to balance my life better.

I also created a vision where I was comfortable not only handling money, but making decisions that people around me might not love regarding money. I pictured myself being able to say *no* and stick to it.

Perhaps most important regarding my money situation, I created a vision where I was in complete, confident control of my money so that I could maintain financial independence regardless of my relationship status.

Step 4: My Plan

Understanding how important it was, I became intent on becoming a well-rounded person with hobbies, interests and to be a life learner. I had to learn how to enjoy my time alone, to do something that I loved when I was single as well as when I was with someone and he wasn't home.

My plan was created so that I could learn how to enjoy life, and become self-reliant, and accept that being away from someone I love does not mean he doesn't love me. It simply means he values himself enough to enjoy his life as much as I value myself. And now, I have a very full life that I love.

I then made it my goal to be financially independent and always know what my finances are and will always be. I decided to stop looking the other way, and tackle my finances head on.

I went online to do research. I read books written by the experts and gathered all the information I needed to make the changes necessary for my vision to become a reality. By learning about finances, I felt more confident and empowered.

First, I wrote down every cost in my life on an Excel spreadsheet. I studied it and learned where I could cut costs, in another words: save money. Next, I monitored my monthly expenses and why they might go up or down weekly. I asked myself with each purchase: *is this a need or a want?*

I learned how to plan for emergencies, most of the time. I created a monthly budget in conjunction with my accountant. And now, if someone asks me what my expenses are, I not only know the answer, I know what I need to earn each month to cover them. I am taking personal responsibility.

Maintaining Your Bounce

The whole point of Bouncing Back Into You is to find a path that will take you out of the low point of your divorce to creating the best life for you possible, the happiest you, the most confident you.

Working through the steps will not take just a few hours on a weekend. You can gain great insight in just a few hours, but to make the lasting changes to fulfill your vision will take much longer. And for each person going through it, it will be such an individual path that no two people will have an identical journey and it will take a different amount of time for every person.

So go easy on yourself in terms of being patient. The work will be painful and tough. Take whatever time you need. And if you find you're losing momentum, remind yourself that the payoff–a happy, confident you–is more than worth it.

Speaking of momentum, one way to keep it going as you work on fulfilling your vision is to create change little by little, snowballing into bigger changes.

For example, perhaps part of your new vision is a leaner, healthier you. You want to look in the mirror, like what you see and feel confident everywhere you go. If you know losing weight is part of that package, then while you work on that, work on smaller, easier parts. Perhaps you start off with something as simple as finding a new shade of lipstick to wear, or just wearing lipstick.

You start looking at yourself in the mirror and notice the change, notice you *like* the change, and it gives you a little boost. Maybe the next thing you do then is get a new hair cut.

Now you see the new you with even more enthusiasm and the motivation to stick to the diet or exercise plan is only increased.

Try it. I promise, if you do something, anything, positive or fun for yourself, it will start some momentum. More positive things will begin to happen, which in turn, will motivate you to discover even more ways to get positive momentum to increase.

Good Days and Bad Days–Remember the Bad Will Pass

It is truly my goal to make sure you are prepared for the ups and downs of divorce or even an end to a relationship. It stinks, but we all survive. Surprisingly for me it was neither divorce that broke my heart; it was a relationship after both divorces that did me in. But, I did bounce back. It was not easy. It took me months, and to be 100% honest as I write this I still think about him and what if?

I cannot *what if* my life to death and neither can you. I am thankful for the heartache it caused because it allowed me to better understand the ups and downs of real, genuine heartache.

The more I think about what is the best advice I can share, it is this: do not go it alone. Please create a favorite list on your phone for your A-team or simply know who your "Go-to Girls" are when you need them most. Being blessed with one or two friends is a gift. It's okay to call a friend and say, I am having a bad day and I need X, whatever the X is: *I need help. I need you to come over and take the kids for a few hours.* Please do not attempt to go it alone – divorce is hard and requires a support system in place. If you do not have a support system, use that as an opportunity to stretch your wings. There are divorce support groups and a variety of counseling centers out there. Reach out to them and ask them to help you find what you need. That's why they are there! There is no shame in having a bad day or in needing help and asking for it. We all need to remind ourselves that people genuinely love to help others.

Chapter 7:
Dating After Divorce

Time to Get Back in the Game

So, you think it's time to get out there in the dating world again? Do me a favor, or wait, do yourself a favor and STOP!

Ask yourself: *is it really time?* What I mean is maybe it's time to figure out what you really want. You know, is it time to date? Or is it just time for sex, you know good old-fashioned one night stands (done safely!)? Or maybe it's just time to put your toe in the water in the big pool of the dating world again and see what it's like "out there."

I like the swim metaphor when it comes to talking about dating because swimming is just like dating. You jump in a pool or lake or dabble on the seashore with hundreds, if not thousands of other people. Some of those people will be fun to play a game with, some will be good to partner off for lap swimming, others are just nice to spend an afternoon with, lounging and relaxing. The same could be said for the dating pool.

So, if it's time to get back in the pool, figure out how you want to do it. You could try slowly on the steps, one step at a time, as you hold tight to the railing. You could dive right in. Or, you can jump into the shallow end and wait until you're comfortable with the water temperature before getting serious with anything. It is all completely up to you. Remember this analogy as you begin your journey back into the dating world. There is a lot, and I mean a lot, of water out there. Just go at whatever pace feels right for you. And one more thing: you would not jump into a pool if you didn't feel comfortable just because your friends wanted you too, right? So please do not start dating just because your friends or family tell you it's time. It is time when you, and only you, are ready. No one knows what is best for you like you do.

It is more than okay to do what's right for YOU! Sexuality should never be taken lightly. We are all human beings and have emotional, spiritual and sexual feelings. I say celebrate those feelings, all of them. I do! I recognize that being a sexual being is important to my soul.

Do spend some time celebrating your new-found sense of independence and singleness! Celebrate being single. In fact, if you have been married for a long time, why not have Single Celebration? We celebrate everything in our society, isn't it time to celebrate you for being brave enough to step back into the wonderful world of singleness?

Time to Think Before You Jump

So yes, feel free to jump back into the dating world when you're ready to. But don't do it without some thought and a realistic perspective, first.

Recently, I was having a conversation with a guy friend. He said: "All the women want to microwave relationships." I thought about that and realized that it's true for both men and women: we all want what we want and fast! It just does not work that way for everyone.

> **If you are newly divorced, my best advice is to give yourself some time. I once met a man for 15 minutes, and I asked him how long he'd been single. He was just divorced, the ink was not even dry on the agreement. Politely, I advised him to take some time to grieve the loss of his marriage and heal from the pain. Yes, we all have pain. I don't care who wants the divorce, we all have pain. Do not try to numb yourself from the pain with another person, alcohol or drugs. Pain is a powerful tool – it teaches us to grow. By facing our pain, we are forced to think about what we can do better and what it really is we need today.**

One of the ways you can develop a realistic perspective on what might work for you is to create what I call a dating plan. By creating a dating plan, you will figure out what, exactly, you're looking for without having to learn from experience.

First ask yourself what is your objective right now?
Think about why you are back in the dating market.

- Do you want to get into another relationship?

- Do you want to play the field to see what's "out there"?
- Are you just looking for sex?

What are your dating goals?

By "goals" I mean, think about the ultimate dating situation: what do you want it to look like?

- What kind of person do you think you would be most comfortable dating? Are religion or politics important to you? What about whether he or she is a parent? What kind of schedule would be a good fit with yours? If you're in the restaurant industry and work most nights and weekends, a person working banking hours might not be a good fit.
- How much time do you have that you're willing to expend on dating? If you are a parent, that means will you consider whether you will only date on the weekends when your kids are with their dad? Are you willing to sacrifice other family or friend time to go on dates?
- Geographically, how far away are you willing to travel to meet dates?

What tools are you going to use to implement the plan?

- Are you going to ask your friends or family members to fix you up on blind dates?
- Are you game for online dating?
- Would you be interested in hiring a match maker?

Of course before you start thinking about any of that, make sure you're certain you're ready to start dating. It may not be your time right now; you may need a break for some alone time first.

You will know when you are ready; **remember it's a journey, not a race.**

Rebound Relationship

Everyone behaves in unique ways when they get divorced. I have witnessed the woman who is broken- hearted, clearly she did not want the divorce and I have seen the other side of the coin: me! I could not wait to leave my first husband.

I remember the night we signed our agreement, I went out with a guy and could not wait to have sex with him. Sex with a new man, other than your ex-husband is like eating a new candy bar that is just bursting with flavor and you cannot savor it fast enough. Sex after being in a miserable situation is so freeing. You feel alive and you think your life is perfect for that moment in time. It can be so intense that you are not willing to give up that man, the new one who made you feel that alive, so you find yourself in what is commonly known as the "rebound relationship." You know, the one you think you cannot live without. The person who made you see that you are desirable and all that good stuff?

It still cracks me up when I think about how much I thought the rebound guy was "the guy." Now, if you are reading this and thinking to yourself, *yup, my guy or gal is my it person*, I say congratulations. But, as I often do, I recommend people to please stop, think and evaluate.

After my rebound guy didn't work out, I hit the online dating world! And, I hit it hard, but safely. I would line dates up, Friday, Saturday and Sunday. The first dates were always the same: for coffee, in a public place and I had an escape plan. But before I talk about online dating, let's clear the air about dating in general.

Lighten Up! I Promise It Gets Better

We must keep our sense of humor throughout the entire dating process. Create a mantra for yourself and live by it. *Not every man is ideal for me; I am ideal for me. Dating is supposed to be fun. I am honoring myself when I say "no."*

This will surely make you laugh: make a goal. I know a woman who told me she knew she wanted to be married. She made a goal to meet a certain number of men by a certain time with her goal to meet her husband. Guess what? It worked.

It's a crazy, fun and often confusing world out there. But it can also be scary and daunting. You need to make an honest assessment to figure out what you want and how to get it. Remember earlier when I spoke about figuring out what you wanted in a marriage? You really need to do that for all relationships. Otherwise you'll wind up dating people who are a waste of your time (or worse).

It is so interesting to watch the cycles of divorce. Most men that I know and have watched go through a divorce, get their "stuff" together after the divorce. They lose the extra belly weight that their ex-wife complained about for so many years. They start to dress nicer, or at least start to care about what they look like. They think it's all fun and games in the beginning. Why wouldn't they? The online world has made it so easy, soooo easy, to find that new perfect sex mate, I mean mate. From Plenty of Fish, Match.com, JDate, eHarmony, you name it it's there. One day, I joked with my friend and said, "I wonder if they have PuertoRican.com?" because I love ethnic men so much. Guess what? They do!

For men, online dating is like being a little kid in a candy store. But, after trying out all the candy, kids will get a stomach ache and they realize it's just not all that it is cracked up to be. Eventually they'll have an epiphany: *ah, yes! This really isn't much fun.* Sure there's plenty of sex. Sex is easy to get for men (and women)! The stuff that really feels good is the super hard part to find.

I have a good-looking male friend at the gym. One day he was bragging about how easy it was for him to get sex. And then he looked at me and said, "But it's getting old." He knew it too: finding the stuff that is real is the hard part.

As I write this, I am still single. I can say with confidence that I have no problem finding a man to sleep with. That is the easy part if that is all I want. I am an attractive, smart, sexy redhead with big boobs, long legs and all I have to do is walk into any bar, smile and go window shopping. Which, by the way, anyone can do. I am not recommending this course of action, I am merely saying you can pick the "man-I-can get for the night" and he's yours for sex.

But, that is not what I want. If that is what you want – go for it. It's okay to know what you want and go for it. Currently, I am divorced for almost six years and I want a healthy relationship with a man who wants to spend the next thirty years with me so we can grow old together.

It's the Most Wonderful Time of the Year!

The holidays as a newly divorced person can be dreadful! Let me say it again, dreadful. I am putting this information right before my online dating tips because online dating has a cycle to it. During the holidays, people tend to feel alone and needy. (I hate the word *needy*, in fact I wish I could just delete it from the English language but it is a reality.) People get needy and a very quiet, creepy, eerie feeling comes over them when they least expect it. BAM! *I am single and OMG it's the holidays!* They feel this rush of adrenaline surging through their bodies–screaming–GET ONLINE! GET ONLINE!

STOP!

Do not give in to the temptation. Pause, reflect and give yourself time. You just might not be ready yet. I wish I would have logged the hours, holidays, weddings, special events etc. that I attended alone so I could prove to you that you will survive just like I did. You will become stronger than you ever imagined you could be. I promise.

Do not romanticize the holidays. Do not watch too many love stories. Stay away from the Hallmark Channel. Instead, write down what you want your future holidays to look like. Maybe even do a map for them. Do anything that will help keep you from thinking you need to find a date for the holidays.

All that you are feeling is normal, and it will go away in time. I promise. Christmas meant a lot to me during my first marriage. It took me years to not associate my ex- with Christmas.

Welcome to the Online Dating World

The online dating world has lost its mind! Imagine this; you have been in a bad relationship for more than five years, now you are free! WOO HOO! You are free. How are you going to meet your next Mr. or Mrs. Wonderful? Well, there are many online dating sites, so I thought I would share my views, or shall I say reviews, of the sites I have been on. I have not tried, nor do I ever see myself trying Tinder, but one never knows where life will lead us. Like my mom always taught me: never say never!

But I did try Jdate, which was crazy for me! I was at the gym running and the man on the treadmill next to me started asking about my dating life. I told him how I was trying Jdate and Match.com. He turned to me and said, "I thought you don't like to date Jewish men?" I said, "I don't." And he replied, "Then why are you on Jdate?" Good question! I went home and deleted my account. It is not that I don't like dating Jewish men (even though I'm Jewish). I have just never had any luck or chemistry with Jewish men. So, note to you, all of you, before you join the sites, do your homework, research, ask around and decide what site seems to match your needs the best.

Personally, I have had, and continue to have, the best luck with Match.com. There is a nice balance of men on the site who seem to fit the profile I am looking for. But here is the secret: it is not a free site. My experience is if it's free, it is not for me, when it comes to the online dating world.

I will openly admit it I tried PlentlyOfFish.com until I could not take it anymore. For me it was simply men wanting sex. They do not hide it, not for a second. I think I am still scarred from a message I once received from a twenty-year-old boy saying *hi* and a few other things I don't feel comfortable repeating here. I responded: *I am sorry did you mean to write to me or did you want me to take you to the liquor store and buy you beer?* And then there were naked men sending pictures to my inbox! So, you see? If you want something in particular, each site has what you want.

While okcupid.com is free, I honestly lost interest in that site early on. I had no luck with eHarmony, I could not even make it though all the questions they ask. I was yelling at the screen on my laptop: "I just want a date, not an investment!" But I guess, if you think about it, if you really want a relationship, there is and has to be an investment. There is an investment of time, energy and commitment. If you have the desire for a relationship, I highly recommend Match.com because of the luck I've had and continue to have on the site, and eHarmony because I do know people who like the screening process, although I think it might be easier to meet with the President than finish all those questions – just for a date.

> **This just in: I joined Tinder as part of my "research" for this book. It is hysterical! You should try it out, too. But beware. It's free and all about how someone looks. The truth is it will probably work for some people, why wouldn't it? Come on, we all know the deal, if we are not physically attracted to someone we are not compelled to talk to them. I have been on now for a few days and I will admit, it's low pressure and easy. If the person you are looking at is attractive to you, you simply touch the heart for like. If you are not attracted to the photo, you touch the X – it's simple as that. There you have it, a quick review of Tinder.**

Online Dating Tips

Regardless of which site you use, here are a few of my online dating tips:

Building Your Profile:

- Only use three photos, maybe four, any more than that looks desperate.
- Make sure your photos are recent. Come on people, we do not need to see what you looked like in your twenties when you are fifty!

- This one cracks me up. Please do not put pictures of you with your ex-girlfriend or boyfriend. Seriously, what purpose do you think it serves?
- No naked shots! I am not kidding–remember this! A picture says a thousand words! If you want the opposite sex to respect you, then show yourself some respect.
- Do not lie about anything, especially your height. If you are going to start any relationship, start out by being honest.
- Decide on what you want, the "must haves" as I call them. I know what I must have for me to date a man.

After you build your profile you can start searching the site to see if there's anyone you think you'd be interested in meeting. Meanwhile, other people will be doing the same thing and looking at you, too. When you find someone, the first step is usually to reach out to that person in a message. My most basic advice here is to keep it honest, short, and polite, yet make yourself sound interesting.

Men:

Here are my top ten tips for what NOT to write in your message (to me anyway). If you put some thought and effort into the email, you may get a response. Here are my top ten worst emails (many I've received more than once) and how I feel about them.

1. Hey. *No! Show me you are willing to put a little effort into it!*
2. Hey baby. *See my response to number 1.*
3. Hi. *Ugh.*
4. Hey sexy. *Ok, so there's more effort. A salutation and a flattering nickname. I hope you read the sarcasm in that statement. Do you really think that's all it takes to make me interested in you?*
5. Good morning gorgeous. *Ditto number 4.*
6. A book. *Wait to give me your life history after you've charmed me enough to meet you. Please, keep your introduction message short and sweet.*
7. You're hot!
8. WOW
9. How's your day going?
10. Nice weather

No, no, no, and um, no.

Believe it or not, in addition to such ultra-short, uninformative messages as above, I have received some pretty aggressive emails from men. Note to all men and women: if someone does not respond, or if he or she responds with a polite, "no, thank you" kind of email, that does not give you the right to attack the person. And if you do, I hope you realize you are assuring that you will never, ever, be given the opportunity to actually meet that person. In fact, I always say to myself, *thank you for the gift of being an ass online and showing me who you are because now I will never respond to you and I will block you from any contact.* Yes, the block option is there for a reason. Don't ever be afraid to use it.

If you are going to take the time to join an online dating site then commit to doing it right, and give your 100% best. Take the time to read someone's profile and write a message that makes sense and will spark their interest, and will hopefully provoke them to write back. Here is a great sample:

Hi Lisa,
Let's laugh our way to a Temple Owls basketball game, enjoy each other's company and end our evening making each other laugh.

This email shows me that he read my entire profile and that he's creative. It also shows that he thought it through.

Remember: we are all busy. Between our work lives, our cell phones, social media and more, the introductory message is supposed to grab the person's attention, not make them hit the delete button.

Women:
Granted, I'm not a man, so I can't say for certain exactly what kind of messages a man wants. However, I have had enough success receiving positive responses from men, that I feel comfortable offering you these pointers for when you send a message to a man through an online dating site.

Before I get to that though, let me say one more thing: READ the entire profile on the man. <u>Yes, read what they have to say.</u> You can learn a lot of information about the men from their photos, things like he's attractive, looks good in green or wears a suit well. But you'll actually learn information about them as *people* if you read their profiles, even the long, and I mean LONG profiles.

OK, now on to what to write about in your introductory message.

1. Look for a something that you are both interested in or have in common. For example, if someone I am writing to likes sports, I will open with a sentence about sports.
2. Always be positive, no one likes a negative email especially when you are trying to make a nice first impression. So no trashing other men on the site. That means, don't say things like *Thank God I finally found someone on this site who might be sane.*
3. Use a nice and original opening. *I enjoyed reading your profile, you seem _____ (fill in the blank with "interesting," "fun," etc.)*
4. If the picture is great, say so!
5. Always end it by inviting a response, such as: *I hope to hear back from you.*
6. And always end on a positive note. I like to say something like: *I hope you are having a nice day and I look forward to hearing back from you.*

The TEXT Game -- What is it all about?

Remember when I said dating was like swimming in one big pool? Be careful when it comes to texting. It's one way to you can drown.

Once you start "meeting" people through online dating sites, you'll discover that the favorite form of communication is texting. Unfortunately with dating, there is no rule book with all the right plays, but I can help you with this one, with texting. And here is my first piece of advice to remember: just because someone is texting you all the time, does not mean you are in a relationship

For some reason, grown men and women like to text, a lot. And, if you ask me, they like to text way too much, especially in the beginning. Personally, I am always impressed with a man who calls and actually wants to talk to me. But, I realize not every woman will agree with me on that and there are plenty who are happy with all the texting. As always, you have to decide what works for you.

However, do not let your relationship become a text fest. I did that after my first divorce. It sounds crazy, but you do eventually feel like you actually know the person through text messages. But you don't!

Be honest with yourself, if you simply want a texting buddy, than embrace your new text buddy. Enjoy the electronic banter and don't forget that that's all it is: banter. You must always be aware of what you want from the communication, otherwise that's what puts you at risk of drowning–in other words, puts you at risk for getting involved in an unhappy relationship should the texting get serious enough for actual phone calls!

I admit a lot can get lost in the text translation, but you can also learn a lot if you pay close attention. Here are a few things I watch for when I'm texting someone new:

- How frequently do they text me during the day? If it is non-stop, the texting not only becomes annoying, but to me it's a red flag that the person feels a need to be connected with me 24/7. He may be the jealous type. He may be needy. Or he may be controlling. Regardless of why, I don't have time for those kinds of men.
- What is their pattern of texting? I can spot if someone is married or maybe in a relationship by their texting patterns. If someone is only texting during work hours, I question why he can only text when he's working. Or sometimes they'll mention they can only text when they are home alone, or only during certain times every day or week, as if they have a schedule. If my gut sends that signal, I am usually right. And the easy trick to determine if I'm right is I'll call them when they least expect it, to see how they react.
- Do they curse a lot in text? That's a big turn off for me. What kind of person engages in gratuitous cursing?
- Does he have rules about texting? If so, are they ones I can appreciate? I once dated a man who would not text me when his kids were around him because they didn't like it when he texted. That told me his kids created the rules in his house. I feel adults should get to decide how they will communicate with other people; it is not the job of their children. To me, the fact he was allowing his kids to dictate his behavior meant he was weak.

A final bit of advice regarding texting is that you should never assume you are the only one the other person is texting. Recently, a newly divorced girlfriend of mine was upset. She had been texting a man for a long while and then finally met him. She thought it all went well, but she never heard from him again. Unfortunately, my girlfriend's experience is not unusual. By texting him, she thought she was getting to know him. But he was texting her to weed through the other swimmers in the pool. After meeting her, he apparently decided she wasn't quite what he wanted, so he moved on.

Just don't ever forget: texting is not a relationship. Only after you both are willing to step out of the pool and actually talk about the two of you in being in a relationship can you then assume you are the only one he is texting or talking too.

...and then there is SEXting

Remember, when I mentioned to think about what you want from your texting communication? Add to that: think about what your texting is saying about you!

Sexting can be fun and I know more people have done it than will admit to it. However, DO NOT start out the communication by sexting right off the bat and then complain that *all he wants is sex* when you are with him. That is hysterical! You just cannot have it both ways.

If you want to date someone, think about the impression you are making on them if you immediately start sexting them. If you start off the "relationship" by sexting, then you are telling them you are just interested in sex. If that is all you're interested in, then fine. But if it's not, then don't sext right away—wait until you're in the relationship before you sext if you really want to.

Time to Meet

I know it can be fun to text, text, text. But eventually you will meet that one man or woman who will peak your interest enough to say–let's meet! The same guidelines and rules can apply to times when a good friend or family member sets you up with someone or when someone you barely know seems attractive and wants to go out with you. The first thing to do is to have that first meeting!

- You must meet the person before you get connected or used to the idea of this person texting you.
- Do not, I repeat, do not tell your entire life story the first time you meet. We all get excited when we are going on a date, okay, maybe I should say nervous, and that means some of us get a little chatty. But seriously, no one needs to know every detail about you the minute they meet you.
- Make a meeting time for an hour, no longer than an hour and, if you can, avoid alcohol! Trust me, I know what I am talking about. If you meet someone for lunch or coffee, you can keep a clear head about you. With wine or a drink, we tend to let our guard down and what we would have taken a pass on all of a sudden looks pretty darn good!

Conversation Starters:

Meeting anyone new for the first time can be nerve racking, even for the best of us extroverts. I thought I would share some of my tips for creating positive conversation during the first meeting and/or date. Remember the first date is NOT where you share your life story and all your deep, dark secrets. The first meeting should really be to see if you want a second date and then you can slowly move forward.

- Current events including sports: Make sure you are prepared, go online and read about the world. Nothing is worse than meeting someone and they have no idea what is going on in the world around them.
- Hobbies: Nothing makes a person more interesting than being well rounded. If you do not have any hobbies, then think about your interests.
- Movies: Have you seen any movies lately? If not movies, what other things have you done recently? Real life as a good conversation starter.
- Talk about anything! Just not the ex!

Remember; people show you who they are very early on, so pay attention. How your date will behave on this first meeting is a good indicator for how he or she will behave on future dates. Trust your gut on your first impressions!

Some Good General Tips

I could write a book just on my funny first dates. I wish I had started a journal when I started my journey as a single woman in my forties. I'm offering the following examples that come directly from my experience. I do so to help you realize what not to do, as well as to offer you a warning of what you might just find:

1. Do not do the ex-spouse talk: Do no talk about the ex- the entire time. No one wants to spend time hearing about your nightmares. No one.
2. Do not text other people: Pay attention and do not text your friends while I am in mid-sentence, seriously, your friends can wait. Everyone should agree to put their phones away.
3. Do not bring up sex! We just met. I have heard it all, from one guy telling me about how his penis is not straight to another telling me how long it had been since he'd had sex.

4. Easy way to turn me off is to bring up marriage: Please do not ask me about my feelings about marriage during our first meeting.

Yes? or No? Be Honest and Kind! Remember, karma, people:
- If you are not interested in following up that first meet-and-greet with an actual date, kindly say so. You don't have to go into a long explanation. Saying *it was so nice to meet you, but I don't think we are both looking for the same things,* will be enough.
- Some people say, (some people) that we should have a few dates to determine if there is something there. I believe you know it or you don't at once. But, this is when I say, *Lisa you have been divorced twice.* So *you* might need to rethink that advice.
- Here is what I truly believe in my heart: Great chemistry is important and for me, if it's not there, it's not there. You can't make it, fake it or pray for it! If it's not there, it's not there.
- I will admit, I have had my fair share of bad first dates, online and set ups. I have tried to be honest and kind. Every now and again I get asked the million dollar request: *really, tell me what you didn't like about me, the truth*. Before I answer, I ask myself, will this help him?

Time for One-Night Stands!

Okay, now when it comes to this stuff–the one-night stand stuff—I may not be the best person to talk about it. I never understood it. It's just not my thing. I was in my forties and had to navigate some new territories when I thought about trying it. I remember asking my friend Kate about one night stands. She's much younger than I and, at that time, I felt she was more experienced with the single world.

I asked, "So who is responsible for bringing the rubber?" She had this odd look on her face as she said, "Lisa, first of all no one calls them rubbers anymore. They are called condoms!"

I cracked up and realized that maybe I was better off not doing the one-night stands.

However, I do realize there are plenty of women who do just want a little sex every now and then with no strings attached. My advice to you is to talk to yourself like you would a teenage: remind yourself of the potential for danger. And make sure that is, indeed, all you want, just sex and that all your partner wants is just sex. As with relationships, honesty is a must!

Romance at Work

There are so many ways to meet someone, online is so just popular and accepted in today's world and I might add, convenient, to the list. However, if you work and are interested in someone you work with – STOP! (I know, I get so excited sometimes when I talk about this stuff!)

Seriously, though, do stop and take the time to really assess the situation. What happens if you date and it works out? What happens if you date and it does not work and now the entire workplace knows about it? This is really a judgment call on your part. For me, when you date someone at work there should be some dating etiquette rules in place.

Consider this: we don't share our personal lives with our fellow workers unless there is something to be shared. So maybe, if you decide to date a coworker, you should apply the same rule. That also means being careful about posting photos on the social media sites. I suggest you wait to make it common knowledge at work until it's more than just dating. Think about it as protecting yourself from people talking about your personal life at the office. You could argue, who cares? Trust me, you should.

If you are going through a divorce *and* you are dating someone at the office, just imagine the rumors that can be created. Remember, in a perfect world people only care about their life, their marriage, and their children. But the world is not perfect. People like to gossip about others. My advice is simple: keep your personal life just that–personal.

First Meeting vs. First Date

I met Richard, my second ex-husband through, friends. Honestly, I think the way they handled it worked perfectly for me. They said, we know a nice guy who we think would be great for you. They asked each of us if we would like each other's numbers and then they stepped out of the fix up, leaving the rest up to us. They were great friends through everything we did–dating, marriage and our divorce.

Richard called me first and we talked–not texted. We talked a few different times and then we decided to meet in person. There is really no right or wrong way to handle the fix up, just the one idea I hold true in all life: always be kind and honest with all parties involved. If you decide to go meet someone based on a friend's recommendation and you don't like him or her, just be honest. Do not feel obligated to go on a second date. In fact, whether you were fixed up or not, you should never feel obligated to meet for a second date if you are not feeling it. It's okay. They are your feelings; own them.

When Richard and I met, we decided to meet at a restaurant in Philadelphia for a drink. It was a casual first meeting and then we made our first date for dinner. A "first meeting" is very different than a first date. The difference is, on a first meeting you're preoccupied with determining whether the person is someone you want to see again. Are they my type? Am I attracted to them? I used to call meetings "drive bys." If there is no physical attraction or connection in your first meeting, what makes you think seeing them a few more times will change that? You and I both know that when there is a connection, it's there and you cannot force it. I am sure there are a few of you shaking your heads and saying she's wrong, then let's agree to disagree. But, for me, I want that connection. I had it once and I am sure I will find it again.

A first date is after the fix up first meeting, or first meeting from online dating. It's when the person asks you out on a proper first date. A good old-fashioned kind of date. You know, where the man opens the door for the lady and you both enjoy an event you mutually agree on such as dinner, a visit to a museum, a baseball game, you get the idea. The date is then spent intent on enjoying each other's company as you continue to get to know each other.

Before Dating

Online dating or just plain dating can be the equivalent of a full-time job. If you decide to make it your job to find "the partner." I have met some wonderful men through online dating and fix ups. I met the first man I ever truly loved, to date that is, online. Please remain hopeful and optimistic. Every person I met served a purpose. Whenever we meet anyone, there is a reason. As my dear, sweet wonderful friend Wendy likes to say, "Every experience we have in the dating world is a stepping stone." When she got divorced after 17 years of marriage, she dated a lot, not because she was looking for "that guy" but because she wanted to see what it was like again to date. Sometimes I think we need to learn to date again.

Going through a divorce is so painful and sad, so please do not go back into the dating world until you are ready.

And think about the logistics. I had mentioned earlier that you should consider creating a dating plan. If you don't feel the need for that, at least take a realistic look at your life and decide how much time you really have to dedicate to dating. If necessary, create a dating schedule.

Take an old-fashioned paper, one-month calendar. Now, write down all of your activities, your kids' activities, work and your childcare schedule. How much time is left? Be honest. You MUST be honest with yourself or this will not work.

Whether you have a limited amount of time or you're pretty open, you won't want to waste your time on the playing field, which is why I have you doing the following exercise: to make a list of some wants from the person you are going to date. For example, here are mine:

1. Flexibility Is Key.
2. Proximity is a Plus: When you add travel to the mix, it is not a deal breaker but closeness does help.
3. Hobbies Help: Having similar hobbies helps. If you are both super busy, but both like to run, then you can incorporate running into your dates.
4. Kids are Cool: How many? What is the custody arrangement? This is an important one to remember, especially if they have younger children, it's not just what weekend? It's how many activities are YOUR kids involved in? For example, my son plays travel baseball, so from June through August I am busy at his games, which are mostly on weekends too.

Keep the Kids Out of the Mix

You get to live by your rules, sex and all. I don't like rules, never did (unless I'm the one writing them). However, for me there are some unspoken rules about dating with kids. Or maybe not so unspoken. Here is one rule or recommendation I have for everyone, though: Keep your kids out of the mix until you know it's for real, that there is something there and you will be together for a while.

No one can predict the future, but your kids have already lived through a divorce, or in my case two, so why do we need to bring them into every new relationship?

My advice, straight from my heart, is this: yes, dating is important, but there is nothing more important than your children. Let's remember that divorce is a confusing, scary time for them. My younger son Ari only met one person I ever dated. We both thought we were going to be together forever. He loved my boys and my boys loved him. Today, I am no longer dating him and now my boys no longer have any interaction with him. When we broke up he mentioned wanting to maintain a relationship with me and the boys. My thought process was, *Why?* We only dated. We were not married. What was there for my boys to gain from them maintaining a friendship with my ex-boyfriend? If we–my ex-boyfriend and I—could not make it as a couple, then why would we be friends when there were so many other feelings involved?

What Does the Ex- Have to Do With it? Pay Attention!

Now, on the other end of the spectrum, I only met my ex-boyfriend's children once. Here is a perfect example of children who were not okay with their parents' divorce and they felt there was no need to have a relationship with their dad's girlfriend. Think about that. It's a critical piece to a relationship.

His children, and his relationship with his children, created a strain on our relationship. It impacts birthdays, holidays and everyday life. It is not easy listening to stories about children who want nothing to do with you. The important part of this is to remember to pay attention to who is truly the decision maker in the mix. I realized early on that my boyfriend at the time was not the decision maker. He was the I-will-do-whatever-it-takes-to-make-sure-my-ex-is-quiet-and-happy person. Because of that, he had no control or say in his children's lives.

I have friends who are dating people with children and they have blended the families together beautifully. It's really important to understand the role the children play, and will always play, in any relationship, dating or long-term. Pay attention.

Another very important detail to consider is this: What is their relationship between the person you are dating and his or her ex-spouse? Don't get overwhelmed, I know I am throwing a lot at you. I am just sharing my thoughts and ideas to help you make it through the dating world and support you as you meet people. I am also sharing my experience to help make yours easier. I have, clearly, been there, done that! So I know, the ex-spouse plays a major role in the dating world, especially if the children live with the ex-spouse who is still harboring hurt and resentment.

So what is your date's philosophy regarding their ex-spouse? What I mean is, how do they talk about their ex-spouse? Listen closely. It's important. Building a relationship with someone, or dating someone can be impacted by their former spouse. If you asked me about either of my ex-husbands here is what I would say: "I truly only want both of them to be happy, and to continue to love their sons and be an integral part of their lives."

Dealing with Your Ex-'s Dating Habits

My boys need their dads. Joe, my first ex-husband, has a lovely girlfriend whom my son Jacob loves. I see that as a major plus for Jacob. Who does not want their children to feel loved and supported by many? Life is hard and the more people that love our children the better. A new person to care about him is truly a bonus.

Richard, Ari's dad, and I are great friends; he loves me and I love him. I am confident when we both settle down with new partners the four of us will not only be friends but we would be comfortable enough to socialize together. I love Richard in a brotherly way. We often joke that we should have just stayed close friends, but if we had done that we would not have our amazing son Ari. Richard is a wonderful person and a terrific dad.

It's my hope that all of us—society at large—realize the seriousness of divorce and the impact it has on our children. Truthfully, I will never really know the impact that both of my divorces had on my oldest son, Jacob. He seems well adjusted and happy. But, how will he handle a relationship? Will he think quitting works? Probably not, but that's because we both spent years in therapy together. There was never a doubt that the divorce had nothing to do with him. We must remind our children that we will always love them and the divorce is not their doing at all.

I don't worry about Ari as much as I do Jacob, since his dad and I get along so well and we co-parent Ari. Richard does introduce Ari to his lady friends. After meeting a few different "friends" we discussed not having Ari meet his "friends" too early on. From my point of view, Ari was getting attached, and then something would happen, and then we would not see them anymore. Richard believed it was okay to introduce Ari to his "friends" early on, but then he realized it is really not necessary to bring Ari into the mix until it's a relationship that will be around for a while.

About the Kids.

Your children learn from you. They watch what you say and do constantly. If you have a daughter, show your daughter that dating is secondary to self love. Teach her what it looks like to date, not what it's like to rush into a relationship that will not sustain itself on SEX alone!

If you have a son, teach him that a woman will not complete him. Teach and show your children how to love and respect themselves in a healthy relationship and then, maybe one day, our divorce rate will be lower. Maybe the next generation will get it right. There are no princes or princesses for anyone to make each other's lives complete in a happily ever after. Teach your children that it's their own job to make their lives great and that a partner just adds the cherry on top!

The Freedom in Dating

Dating when you are divorced with children can have its fair share of challenges, but never forget dating is way more fun after you have your children. Did you ask yourself if you want more kids? Me, I am good with two. So, my biological clock is done. My career is great. So, now I get to date.

It's funny, but when you are older, you get to have way more fun. You have the money to do more, experience more, and live without the pressure of getting married. This is the time of your life to say: this time is all about me. I will date if I want to, I will date who I want to, and most importantly I am NOT in a race to walk down the aisle, I am simply looking to enjoy life and find my partner and live for today.

I have a theory that I think it is time to share with you. Dating, once you have your goals and schedule created, is like eating ice cream at Baskin-Robbins Ice Cream. Remember that ice-cream parlor who gave us thirty-one favors? If you have been married for a long time, let's say you have been enjoying vanilla ice-cream, dating gives you the opportunity to explore other flavors. Embrace the fact that you are a new YOU! Do not keep eating the same flavor of ice-cream. It's time to change it up!

Think of dating as an extra once you have your house and life in order. It's just a way to expand your world. Remember, there are all kinds of ways to meet people to date. I met my first husband when I was working as a waitress and he was a customer. You simply do not know when or where you will meet someone. I featured online dating and fix ups, because that is how I have met men in the dating world most recently. But there are many other ways: join a Meet Up group, become a volunteer, follow your passion.

Just try to be patient, I know it can be hard and it gets lonely and often scary. Sometimes you'll find yourself worrying about being single forever. When you do, take a deep breath, sit back and use your singleness to create happiness.

One Day

I am very optimistic that one day I will meet someone who will love me as I am and I will love them as they are for the next 30 years. YES! That is my goal. Currently, I am having the time of my life loving me for me. My life has never had more meaning or felt so fulfilled, but as a close friend of mine says, "I am simply looking for the icing on my cake." I have the foundation of a wonderful life so I say, "When I find that relationship it will be the cherry on top of the sundae," to mix metaphors.

Love is hard work. It's not what the movies and TV shows of my childhood taught me it is supposed to look like. It's when a man and a woman are best friends and are always there to support each other through the good, the bad and sometimes, the ugly. It's a partnership. When two people are together, it makes them better. They work together to create their own universe within this universe. I am clear that the next person I commit to being in a relationship with is going to be my friend first. My last boyfriend and I were best friends and we had some really good ingredients for a long-term relationship. Notice the word, *some*. We did not have them all because if we did, we would still be together. At my age, I am looking for all of the ingredients to be in place. Most importantly, I want someone who wants to grow together and work hard to make the relationship strong and ever-lasting.

Friends, best friends and then lovers, to think for so many years I had it WRONG! Well, like the expression goes–better late than never (or is it better late than pregnant).

74

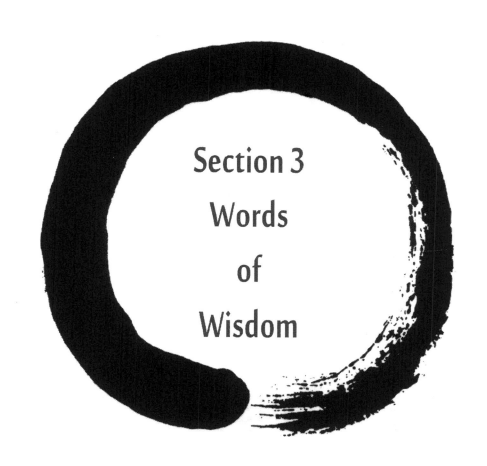

Section 3
Words
of
Wisdom

Chapter 8:
Legalities and Finances of Divorce

Since my area of expertise is not finance or legal matters and I wanted to write a complete guide to help you through your divorce, before, during and after, I went to the experts: Lynda Hinkle and Catherine Allen. These two ladies are truly experts in their fields. They were both generous enough to offer the best advice they have in their respective fields.

Before I turn it over to Lynda Hinkle for some legal advice though, I want to say this: make sure you like your divorce attorney. I know Lynda offers this advice too and it's true. You will be spending time with them and it is very much like any relationship. It needs to based on one trust and respect. If you do not feel comfortable with them from the start, then do not sign with them. One more piece of advice is this: do not skimp on your attorney. My first divorce attorney was expensive, but like the saying goes, you get what you pay for. My first attorney was aggressive, smart and on top of my case. She always made me feel that I was a priority to her. She was responsive and truly, truly made me believe she was fighting for me and what I needed.

My second divorce attorney was a referral from a friend, who was "doing me a favor" by cutting his retainer fee and promising my friend he would take great care of me. Well, to be honest he was not the best attorney and I never felt like he cared. I always left his office feeling like I was just another client. My first attorney was caring, compassionate and really made me believe that she cared about the final result and outcome. She was what I hope every divorce attorney is for all of their clients.

HELPFUL HINTS FROM A DIVORCE LAWYER

By: Lynda L. Hinkle, Esq.

The legal process of divorce can seem overwhelming and perhaps even almost as painful as the actual break up. There are ways, however, that you can maximize the success of your outcome and minimize the hassle and expense. Below are a few tips for navigating your divorce successfully through the legal process.

1. Choose a good lawyer. Selecting a lawyer is one of the most significant decisions you will make as you progress through the divorce process. A good divorce attorney provides clear, helpful legal advice, intelligent advice, and a modicum of practical support through the process. Trust your instincts. If you aren't sure that a lawyer is right for you, don't settle for them even though Aunt Suzy loved them, or they have great online reviews. Every case is different and every person is different, so find a lawyer whose personality and style fits yours and your situation.

2. Arm the lawyer not just with facts but also with what your ultimate wishes are. I advise clients to take time out before beginning the divorce process to write a list of everything they want to take out of the marriage, and then rank order them. You will not win everything. Family court is built to make everyone lose something, so expect that will happen. Decide what are your top 3-5 things that are worth sacrificing all the others for. Provide your lawyer with this list and also with all the facts, even if they aren't very flattering, so they can do their job well.

3. Trust your lawyer, but don't rely on them alone. Your lawyer is not your accountant, financial advisor, therapist or best friend. They are your lawyer. Have those other people ready to help you in the unique way they are positioned to do so.

4. However, trust your lawyer, not laymen, when it comes to law. Nothing drives lawyers more crazy than someone coming to them reporting what their friend at work or their cousin got in their divorce. First, people lie: maybe they got more alimony, but they may not be telling you the whole truth about their financial position which may be much, much different than yours. Secondly, every case is different...and what people are willing to negotiate based on their circumstances isn't the same as what the law will require of them if the matter goes to trial. If your lawyer is telling

you the law in your state doesn't favor you getting the same alimony result as Cousin Jude, she probably knows what she is talking about.

5.   Be reasonable in your approach, don't corner anyone. Some people think that they can "win" divorce negotiations by continuing to push just to hurt the other person when they have already achieved results better than what they might get at trial. It is rarely wise to risk a good negotiated deal because you really want to stick it to your spouse and force them into a corner on an issue that you know is not as important to you but is crucial to them. Ladies, if he wants the 50 inch television, let him have it if it means you will get more than 50% of the house. Buy your own TV. And gentlemen? Just cause she cheated on you does not mean that you get to withhold 50% of the pension accrued during the marriage, and fighting over well established law just because you are mad is not doing you any favors.

6.   Consider the impact of your decisions on your children and your future. Think about how you in six months will feel about the decisions you are making now. Can you live with them? Have you considered the impact on your children of insisting on a particular parenting time schedule? Or what life may be like for you when this has all settled down and you go on to a more normal routine?

7.   Let your lawyer do the talking: not your anger, not social media. Don't fight with your spouse anymore. Just don't. If you can't agree on something, unless it's an urgent issue involving your children, let the lawyers handle it. Also, keep it off Facebook. Please. Because finding a furious Facebook post in the exhibit list of the other side is not a good thing.

8.   Be clear what your financial goals and impact are. Make sure you have written out a budget and what you need to go on with your life. If it's going to take more money than you have to keep that house, maybe you should sell it. If it's going to be too expensive to maintain that time share, let the other side have it. Know what you need, what you can afford, and what you can do without in the long term and communicate that to your lawyer.

9.   Manage the use of your lawyer economically. If your lawyer has staff that cost less than speaking to them, use that liberally. Also, talk to your lawyer about the things that matter, but

don't use them as a counselor or insist on talking to them at every step in the process unless you have unlimited funds to pay them.

10. When it's all over, try to make sure it's all over if you can. The best way to do this is negotiate a deal that both parties can live with and that lawyers have written up very clearly. Then abide by it and try to be civil, so that you don't end up having to call that lawyer and plunk down some more money for post-divorce motions and issues. Try to develop a working relationship with your ex- if you have outstanding issues, such as children, a business or debts. You don't have to like them. But being able to work with and communicate with them can make all the difference in your future.

THINK FINANCIALLY, NOT EMOTIONALLY

By Catherine B. Allen, CERTIFIED FINANCIAL PLANNER™

Whether you are preparing for divorce, in the process, or have finalized the divorce, there are a range of emotions you may feel: anger, heartache, fear, loneliness, guilt, vulnerability, depression, or perhaps relief. You may feel overwhelmed and not know where to begin when it comes to getting your financial life in order. I have spoken to many women that let their husbands handle all the financial decisions—or at least the big ones, like their retirement planning and investing— while the women handled the day to day finances like bills and children's expenses. How can you possibly take care of the children, manage their busy schedules, manage the household, pay the bills, and perhaps work outside of the home, and be expected to handle the investing and saving for retirement and college? I'm overwhelmed just writing about it!

Consider the story of Debbie, who I heard about from a friend. (Her name and some details have been changed). Debbie was married to Rich for 20 years, has two sons, a gorgeous home, nice cars, vacationed at the shore for most of the summer, and just recently started working part-time. She has a college degree in teaching but when the children were growing up, she and Rich decided she would stay home and he would be the bread winner. Life, for the most part, was great.

Rich worked for a large corporation but decided to work for himself and became self-employed about ten years ago. He worked from home and handled his business and their "big" financial planning. Debbie paid the bills, took care of the house, chauffeured the children around all their sporting events, lacrosse, swimming and boy scouts, had dinner on the table every night, and made sure everyone was happy. If the family was happy, then Debbie was happy.

When Debbie started working part-time she enjoyed her job and loved the interaction with the other employees. Due to her schedule she usually missed the mail delivery, so Rich would leave it in a pile for her on the kitchen counter. Debbie, now working and still maintaining the household and children, didn't pay attention to the fact that she never saw bank or financial statements with the other mail. As a matter of fact, Debbie thought in hindsight, she doesn't even remember ever seeing the tax returns or signing them for that matter. But hey, that was Rich's job and after 20 years of marriage, she trusted him completely. Oops. I think you have an idea of where this story is going.

Rich went away for a few days to visit some old college buddies in Virginia. Debbie received the mail and as fate would have it, the one time Rich is away, a letter from the IRS is staring her in the face. They owed taxes and penalties for not filing for the past five years. Are you kidding me? Debbie is very cautious with money, always kept to a budget, and made sure their household bills were paid on time. How could this have possibly happened? Her mind started racing, her knees became weak, she felt dizzy, sick to her stomach, and almost fainted. Once she recovered from the initial shock she did something smart – she called her father instead of Rich. Her thought was if Rich lied about filing their tax returns, then what else was he lying about? What would he do if she confronted him?

When Debbie did confront Rich, he became very angry and defensive, and as she told her friend, he looked straight into her eyes and continued to lie. Their mortgage hadn't been paid in months, the tax return was never filed, so no taxes were paid, the college tuition was overdue, and there was nothing left in Rich's IRA.

Debbie was fortunate to have the love and support of her family and children and was able to pull herself together and organize her thoughts. If I met with Debbie, I would give her the following checklist of what she needed to do to prepare for divorce, during the divorce process, and after the divorce is finalized. Now I will share that information with you.

PREPARE FOR DIVORCE

Put together a team to work on your behalf and have them connect with one another (i.e. Attorney, Financial Advisor and CPA). I strongly recommend that you meet with your Financial Advisor *before* the divorce is final so she can put together an analysis of your finances and work with your Attorney to optimize the best division of marital property, which includes assets that you may not even know you are entitled to (for instance, his company retirement plan and pension, if he has one). I cannot tell you how many women I have spoken to that just want to get the divorce over with and agree to whatever the ex-husband is offering. I have some news for you...your soon-to-be-ex-husband's best interests are usually exactly opposite of yours. Don't ever assume you are not entitled to assets that are just in his name such as property, investments, stock options, etc. In a divorce settlement, you need to make sure you are dividing assets that are best for short term and long term financial security. Receiving the house and not receiving part of his retirement assets could be a huge detriment to your financial future and the difference between struggle and stability. Remember, think financially and not emotionally!

The second step in preparing for divorce is to gather important documents such as brokerage statements, bank statements, property titles, insurance policies, tax returns, mortgage, & retirement plan (i.e. 401(k) and IRAs).

Obtain a copy of your credit report and resolve any credit issues. You can check your credit score by requesting your credit report for free from annualcreditreport.com. If your ex-husband is responsible for a debt, include an indemnity clause in the divorce settlement in the event of a default. Also, regardless of state, your name should not be taken off property deeds or titles if your name is on the loan. However, if your ex-husband is keeping any property, any loans should be refinanced in his name.

The next step when meeting with your Financial Advisor is to estimate your living expenses and establish a realistic budget. Having a budget is the core of proper financial planning and well-being.

DURING THE DIVORCE PROCESS

There are several steps you should take during the divorce process.

First, know whether you live in an "equitable distribution" or "community property" state. If you live in a community property state you and your spouse must split any marital assets equally. However, if you live in a state that requires equitable distribution, assets must be divided equitably (fairly) rather than equally. Property is also classified as either separate property or marital property so it's important to know how your state classifies property. For example, one state may mandate that separate property consists of gifts, inheritances, and property owned prior to the marriage, and that such items will not be divided between the spouses in the event of a divorce. Another state may proclaim that all property owned by the couple is marital property, subject to division at divorce – it doesn't matter who inherited what. Your attorney will help you make this determination.

Don't shortchange yourself by overlooking hidden assets. For instance, you may know your joint savings account balance and what possessions you must divide, but do you know the balance of your husband's pension plan? Does your husband own a prepaid life insurance plan? Does your husband have retirement funds with his employer (i.e. 401(k)) or IRA's? I had heard of a story of a husband who bought a house in Florida with his "girlfriend" while he and his wife were getting divorced. Fortunately, the wife's attorney hired a forensic CPA who uncovered this asset and it became part of the divorce settlement. Bottom line – BE AWARE that there could be assets you didn't even know about.

The second step, if necessary, is to obtain a temporary order for spousal and child support.

Third, review your proposed settlement with your Financial Advisor prior to signing on the dotted line. It is beneficial that I meet with clients and their attorney before the divorce is finalized to make sure the financial assets are properly divided.

Fourth, find out what the impact would be if you sold your home before or after the divorce.

Another important step is to ask your CPA if it would be beneficial to finalize the divorce next year so you could file jointly one last time.

Lastly, ensure that you'll have continued healthcare coverage. If you're covered under your husband's plan you'll have to obtain new insurance to avoid a gap in coverage.

AFTER THE DIVORCE IS FINALIZED

Now it's all about you. Yes, your children as well if you have them, but what I mean is your life has changed and now is the time to get off the emotional rollercoaster and reevaluate, and perhaps significantly change your saving and spending habits. The choices and decisions you make will have a deep impact on the rest of your life (especially financially!).

Planning now could help provide you with a sense of financial empowerment. Let's go over some steps to get you on the right track.

Step One - Schedule an appointment with your Financial Advisor to review and adjust your portfolio as necessary. Some of the investments that were in your joint accounts or in your ex-husband's retirement accounts may not be appropriate for you. If you had met your Financial Advisor prior to the divorce, then she should already know what your risk tolerance is, as well as your overall objective for your assets. A written financial plan is crucial to knowing where you are financially and how to get where you need to be for the future, short term and long term. What may have been suitable for your ex-husband may be completely wrong for you!

Step Two - Revise your will. Your will determines how your estate is to be distributed upon your death. Along with updating your will, you should also change any medical directives and powers of attorney.

Update your beneficiary designations. If you have any retirement accounts, whether your own IRA or a retirement plan held through your employer, make sure your beneficiaries, primary and contingent, are named per your instructions. It is important that you name people versus your estate as your beneficiary. One of the worst things you can do is name your estate as your beneficiary. Ideally your IRA should not pass through your estate. However, if your beneficiaries are not properly named, or your beneficiary form cannot be located, then it will pass through your estate. In that case, it will be distributed per the instructions in your will, but will become subject to probate.

What's the problem with probate? Well, your IRA will then be subject to creditors and taxes which will reduce the amount you intended to leave to your beneficiaries. There could be other legal complications as well.

Additionally, if your estate is named as beneficiary, you can no longer use any distribution strategy that is based on life expectancy, because an estate is not a person in the eyes of the law. Most likely the IRA will be paid out in lump to your estate, eliminating the opportunity to continue accumulating any earnings on a tax-deferred basis.

Naming beneficiaries also applies to life insurance policies, bank certificates of deposit, investment accounts and any other accounts that allow a beneficiary to be named. For instance, investment accounts use the term "Transfer on Death" (TOD) but you must request it when opening the account.

Step Three – Obtain or modify health insurance coverage.

Step Four – Make sure you obtain new property and casualty insurance for your home, car, etc. You may also talk to your insurance agent about purchasing an umbrella policy for additional protection against liability.

You should also discuss with your Financial Advisor if you should purchase additional disability insurance and long term care insurance at the current time or in the future.

Step Five – Open an IRA Rollover account with your Financial Advisor to transfer the retirement assets, if any, that you received through the divorce settlement. The legal term is Qualified Domestic Relations Order (QDRO) that transfers retirement assets to an ex-spouse after the divorce is final. These transfers are not subject to early withdrawal penalties, however, transfers must be made directly from one retirement account (his 401(k)) to the other (i.e. your IRA) to avoid a 20% withholding tax.

Knowledge is power. It is important to take control of your finances and learn what you need to do in order to be financially healthy. Do not be afraid to ask questions and truly understand what is suitable for your comfort level. With knowledge comes confidence that will help you make the right decisions. If you feel you have made educated choices and decisions, you will have peace of mind that you are directing your own financial security. And that, my friend, is empowering!

With over 29 years of experience in the financial industry, Catherine is deeply compassionate and driven to educate and empower people to make informed decisions in their financial lives. She is a CERTIFIED FINANCIAL PLANNER™ Practitioner trained to develop and implement comprehensive financial plans for individuals, businesses, and organizations. She has the knowledge and skills to objectively assess your current financial status, identify potential problem areas, and recommend appropriate options. Catherine is not a lawyer or a tax professional, so please consult with your advisors before taking any action. Securities offered through LPL Financial, Member FINRA/SIPC. Financial planning offered through M

Financial Planning Services, a Registered Investment Advisor and separate entity.

Chapter 9:
Final Advice

Basic Business—Keep Your Divorce Out of the Office

It's so hard not to run to the office and vent to your colleagues on a daily basis about how your ex- did this or your ex- did that. I will let you in on a secret: your work family loves you and cares about you, but they do not want to hear about your stuff every day. Honestly, do yourself a favor and limit the amount of time you want to talk about your divorce anywhere, especially at the workplace, or you will quickly become the person everyone wants to ignore.

I am not being mean. I am being honest. I am a professional who knows this to be very true. Let's keep it real, workplace friends love their workplace family but no one likes the person who is always talking about negative stuff. If asked how the divorce is going, simply respond with, "It's moving forward." That's easy and requires no lengthy explanation. Remember, less is more and man, oh man, did I need to learn that lesson.

Learn from me, practice some good business etiquette and it will pay off dearly in the long run. You do not want your manager to say, "I wish I could promote her, but it seems like it is a bad time with her going through the divorce and all her personal problems."

It's All So Social!

It may be easy to keep your divorce on a limited, need-to-know basis, but social media is a whole other monster.

We all love social media, okay, maybe not everyone, but I do. Keep in mind all the social media warnings we tell our kids: what you put "out there" can stay there forever.

Social media can be a double-edged sword. On the one side, you can (and I hope you do) be friends on things like Facebook with your ex-, but only if you can be an adult. You know what I mean. It will be hard in the beginning, but as time moves on and the pain dims, you will see that being friends with your ex-partner can go a long way.

On the other side of the sword, though, social media can have far reaching effects if you're friends with your ex- and there is hatred or animosity. One time I dated someone who was friends with his ex- on Facebook. She watched his Facebook page and mine like a hawk. I had no idea who she was in the beginning. I called him and asked: "Who is X? She comments on every post."

She was his official Facebook stalker. No, wait! She was his life stalker. And, she started stalking my pages, too. She once caught him out with me by checking out my Instagram account. Just to be clear: they were divorced for years! She just thought she was entitled to know and control his whereabouts. She's one of reasons we are not together anymore.

My Final Wish and Message for You

I told my publisher that I wanted to launch this book the week of February 14, Valentine's Day, because I wanted you to know that a break up of a marriage or a relationship is all survivable. I believe it so much that when I told my friends I was launching the book the week of Valentine's Day, my one friend replied and said, "that makes sense since you were married the first time on Valentine's Day."

Her words literally stopped me in my tracks. I had forgotten my first wedding date! Totally wiped it out of my mind and yet I remember the first Valentine's Day we were not together and it felt like the end of the world. Guess what? It wasn't. Divorce is not a terminal disease that will take your life; it's an end that leads to a wonderful new beginning.

I hope you enjoyed reading this book as much as I enjoyed putting it together for you. You know you are not alone in this journey – there are so many people that love and care about you. If you need help, please do not be afraid to reach out and get it. There are so many wonderful support groups available – just know you do not have to go it alone. For most of my adult life I believed that going it alone meant showing strength and resolve. It does not mean that at all, it means letting your pride get in the way and not knowing when to ask for love and support. I hope you will learn from my lessons and refer back to the book when you need too.

Life is an incredible journey filled with ups, downs and all-arounds. Being divorced twice has made me a better person and most importantly a better partner, one who understands the level of commitment and work required to keep the relationship strong.

Now, as you prepare to go on the best journey of your life, I have what I hope are some inspiring thoughts for you. I asked a few people to share their stories to help anyone who is reading this book remember that they are not crazy! We have all been there! Done that!

I hope you will take some of the advice they offer and then truly make your new life the best it can be. Remember, when life happens, bounce back!

Chapter 10:
Stories to Share

As promised, here are a few short stories from women talking about their lives and how they survived during and thrived after their divorces. (Editorial note: the following information comes directly from each source with only minor editorial adjustments to ensure clarity.)

Meet Val

Current age: 40
Number of years married: 9
Age at the time of divorce: 36
Were there any children involved? If so, how old were they at the time of the divorce? Yes, one child who was 7 years old.

Her story

My ex husband and I had troubles 3 years before our separation. I suggested therapy but he was worried that it would drive us further apart. I had been contemplating leaving for months, maybe even a year. I do not believe either one of us was 100% in the right or wrong. It always takes 2 people to make or break a relationship. We had some pretty bad fights and I was the one who resorted to alcohol to hide and numb the pain. I am not a pleasant drunk so I'm sure you can imagine some of the fights.

Anyway, I come from parents who have been together since they were in high school so divorce was not a common thing. I have learned that for most people, it's easier to find someone else and use that as your excuse to leave than it is to tell the person you are with you are leaving. For me, I sought out a friendship which later turned into a relationship with another man. My ex- and I lived in the same house for months, yet slept in separate bedrooms. I will say, it was not easy nor comfortable. When the time came for me to move out, it was one of the most challenging days of my life. Not because I wanted to stay married, rather because of the fear associated with the loss I was starting to experience. See, most people think it's going to be easy and better. In a lot of cases, it will be better but only if you work on it. People, including myself, don't realize the grief involved with getting a divorce. You don't just divorce your spouse but you divorce their family, their friends, the friends both of you have accumulated over the years and the life you once knew. I still miss some of the friends I had when I was married to him. People don't know what to do with you when you go from being a couple, to being two entities away from one another.

My ex- and I were committed to not spending a fortune with knock-down-drag-out fighting via the attorneys. We chose to pursue the mediation route. It was probably the best decision we made. We still had to have an attorney finalize everything and we had to go to court but it didn't take years, rather it took months. Please don't mistake that there were not issues that caused some heat and tension but we tried to make sure we kept our son's best interest in mind.

Biggest challenges:

The biggest challenge was the fear of starting all over again. How, what do I do, who am I, and am I a good mother? The guilt was something that weighed heavily on me for years.

Have you since remarried?

Yes, I did remarry and so has my ex-husband. Interestingly, we lived a block and a half away from one about for about a year and a half. It made it very easy on our son as he could walk back and forth between the two homes.

If you could give just one piece of advice to someone about to go through divorce, what would it be?

Don't put your kids in the middle. It's not their fault mom and dad didn't make it work. Don't use them as pawns in your game. You are the adults, step up and act like it.

In what ways are you better for the experience?

Wow, I am a completely different person for the better having come through the experience. I went to therapy to not only help me get over the grief but also work on my issues. I stopped drinking as I knew it was not in my best interest or that of my child to continue consuming alcohol. I also get along very well with not only my ex-husband but his wife as well. I couldn't ask for a better woman to be a mom to my son when I'm not around. I've learned that holding on to anger and resentment only hurts you, not the other person.

Meet Marlene
Current Age:
Number of Years Married:
Were there any children involved? If so, how old were they at the time of the divorce? 16-19-22
Her Story:
Very amicable divorce promising husband to be there for him if we ended peacefully. Suffered severe anxiety and refused to take medication.
Biggest challenges:
Money. I was responsible for college bills. No alimony or child support. I paid him to keep the house.
Have you since remarried?
Remarried several years later and have been married almost 15 years.
If you could give just one piece of advice to someone about to go through divorce, what would it be?
Mediate, it's the way to go. Attorney bills add up, And try to plan your divorce in advance of filing.
In what ways are you better for the experience?
Better because of the dead weight of living with extreme negativity is gone. I got my mojo back.

Meet: Faith
Current age: 47
Number of years married: 8
Age at the time of divorce:
Were there any children involved? If so, how old were they at the time of the divorce? One son. 6.

Her Story:

The divorce itself was fairly short. I filed in January 2003. It was complete October 2003. For this we want to speak: the story is amicable but complicated.

It almost was like mediation but with lawyers

Biggest challenges:

Starting over. Very different being divorced with child. You are caught between two worlds. Single life and the marrieds but without family unit.

Have you since remarried?

No

If you could give just one piece of advice to someone about to go through divorce, what would it be?

Keep it about the two adults and moving forward. Keep kids out. It ends up better.

Also no matter how good or bad a divorce is, it us still very difficult and taxing even after a long period of time.

In what ways are you better for the experience?

More adventurous. Developed many new interests. Got master's won awards serve on boards. Professional growth. And, very important: Quality time, more meaningful time related to my son. Every second counts.

Meet: Jo-Ann

Current age:

Number of years married: 13

Age at the time of divorce: 38

Were there any children involved? If so, how old were they at the time of the divorce? 2 children - Boy 9 and Girl newborn

Her Story:

Ex- was very uncooperative. It took 2-3 years to settle financially. I had to give up much of what he owed. Still worth it. I remember thinking I am alone with two children and will have nothing, BUT I thought at least I will have my own peace and not this constant fighting, berating, verbal abuse. So I decided it was the right thing.

Biggest challenges:

Financial, No other family members to help so fear of money, illness, consequently.

I kept a tight rein on pay checks and lived simple quiet life. Stuck to a budget—accounted for every penny. I remember even when I got furniture, I could not put things together but I didn't pay anyone else to do it. My son at 9 or 10 stepped in to help me with everything to include bringing in Christmas tree, putting furniture together, getting little jobs to help himself. He is now a grown man doing well.

I know the constant verbal fighting of my first marriage affected the children negatively even to this day.

Have you since remarried?

Yes

If you could give just one piece of advice to someone about to go through divorce, what would it be?

1) Keep the children out of the differences between you and your ex-. Find common ground between you and your spouse to agree that the children should not suffer the pain of your anger or become pawns between you. That's the biggest. Here are a few more.

2) Be realistic about custody and finances .

3) Seek guidance regarding finances or if you can't do that, set up a budget and stick to it.

4) Consider you can't know today what your children will need in 15 years when negotiating an agreement so keep that in mind,

5) Work with an attorney who can specifically answer your questions and who has your best interest at heart.

In what ways are you better for the experience?

I am in a happy marriage now. I refused to live my life victimized nor let my children see that as a role model. I am free to be who I am and do what brings my family and me joy.

Meet: Marcianne

Current age: 56

Number of years married: 1st marriage was 6 years, 2nd marriage was 4 years

Age at the time of divorce: I was 33 at the time of my first divorce. I was 46 at the time of my second divorce

Were there any children involved? If so, how old were they at the time of the divorce? I had two children from my first marriage and they were ages 4 and 2 at the time of the divorce. I had no children with my second husband and my kids were ages 17 and 15 at the time their step-father and I divorced

Her Story:

Divorce, in my experience, is gut wrenching and heartbreaking.

Biggest challenges:

Getting back into the workforce after being a stay-at-home mother.

Have you since remarried?

I remarried after being single for 8 years (which felt like 80 years).

I have not remarried since my second divorce and doubt that I will. Not need. Companionship, love and sex? Yes. Legal bond? Not so much. ;-)

If you could give just one piece of advice to someone about to go through divorce, what would it be?

Don't spend time and energy rehashing your grievances or worrying about your ex-'s happiness or, more likely, his hoped-for misery. Instead, use that time and energy to care for yourself and your children. Caring for yourself includes the hard work of rebuilding your life, e.g. regaining your confidence, establishing a support system, building a career, and the incidentals.

In what ways are you better for the experience?

I am better for the experiences in many, many ways. My heart was broken but a broken heart is more open and compassionate. I became self-reliant. I gained a strong sense of self-worth by accomplishing so many things I never would have attempted if not for the divorces. I learned forgiveness on a deep, resonant level. I didn't forget, but I forgave. I found a spiritual practice that comforted me and enlarged me beyond my wildest dreams. I found my talents and learned to accept my weaknesses with grace. I learned gratitude for what is, while giving up whining about and pining for what just was not meant to be. I finally grew up!

Acknowledgements

A special thank you always goes to my parents for their unconditional love and support. Without my family and all of their love, I know I would have never made it to where I am today. I am truly blessed with an amazing support team including my aunt Roberta, Uncle Ted, cousin Jodi, my brothers Larry and Michael, and my wonderful sisters-in-law Laura and Tisa.

We all know I could write a book about my friends and how fortunate I am to have such richness in my life! To all of my friends who have always helped me bounce back, I say, "Thank you for being part of my life, my team and my heart. I treasure all of you."

This last thank you goes to Lisa Shiroff, my editor, my publisher and now, someone I call a friend. Lisa is my sunshine. Her influence in my life has been life changing for me. Since the day we met she has kept me on my toes, pushed me, challenged me and most importantly makes me better with every phone call, text and email. Together, I know we will continue create books that help people bounce back from life's adversity.

About the Author

Motivational speaker and marketing entrepreneur **Lisa Bien** knows finding success in any area of life requires self confidence and perseverance.

After twenty years of creating successful marketing strategies and public relations campaigns, and in addition to her continuing role as President of B!EN MARKETING GROUP, Lisa is now bringing her trademark energy and passion for storytelling to a more personal level. Lisa regularly serves as a keynote speaker, holds personal development workshops, coaches business professionals, is an author, and hosts her own TV show and YouTube channel: BounceBackLisaBien.

To learn more about Lisa, about her upcoming appearances, the TV shows, coaching services and to sign up for her newsletter, please visit her Bouncing Back website at:

www.LisaBien.com

19294775R00065

Made in the USA
Middletown, DE
14 April 2015